Prove It!

Using Textual Evidence

Levels 3–5

Melissa Cheesman Smith
Terri Schilling
Foreword by Alan Sitomer

Inset worksheet page:

Name _____ Date _____   LESSON 4

INDEPENDENT PRACTICE

"The Key"

Directions: Read the question at the bottom of the page. Then, read the passage. Annotate and highlight while reading to help you answer the question. Include a cited quotation to support your answer.

The Key—Adapted from *The Secret Garden* by Frances Hodgson Burnett

Mary looked at the key a long time. She wondered if it was the key to the closed garden. If she could find out where the door was, perhaps she could open it and see what was inside the walls. It was because it had been shut up so long that she wanted to see it. It seemed as if it must be different from something strange must have happened there over the years.

She isn't sure where the door is.

She put the key in her pocket and began to walk. No one but herself ever seemed to come there. She could walk slowly and look at the wall, or rather at the ivy growing on it. The ivy was the baffli... looked, she only saw thickly growing, gloss... disappointed. Something of her contrarin... walk and looked over it at the treetops inside... to be near it and not be able to get in. She took the key in her... back to the house. And she made up her mind that she would a... her when she went out. If she ever found the hidden door, she...

1. Why can't Mary use the key to get into the closed garden.

_____

_____

_____

Tip: Be sure your answer has three parts: an answer... question, a quotation and in-text citation, and a summary with a connection or explanation.

Publishing Credits

Corinne Burton, M.A.Ed., *Publisher*; Conni Medina, M.A.Ed., *Managing Editor*; Emily R. Smith, M.A.Ed., *Content Director*; Veronique Bos, *Creative Director*; Shaun N. Bernadou, *Art Director*; Stephanie Bernard, *Associate Editor*; Courtney Roberson, *Senior Graphic Designer*

Image Credits

All images from iStock and/or Shutterstock

Standards

© 2014 Mid-continent Research for Education and Learning
© Copyright 2010. National Governors Association Center for Best Practices and Council of Chief State School Officers. All rights reserved.
© Copyright 2007–2017 Texas Education Association (TEA). All rights reserved.
ISTE Standards for Students, ©2016, ISTE® (International Society for Technology in Education), iste.org. All rights reserved.
© 2007 Teachers of English to Speakers of Other Languages, Inc. (TESOL)
© 2014 Board of Regents of the University of Wisconsin System, on behalf of WIDA—www.wida.us

Shell Education

A division of Teacher Created Materials
5301 Oceanus Drive
Huntington Beach, CA 92649-1030

http://www.tcmpub.com/shell-education
ISBN 978-1-4258-1700-8
©2018 Shell Educational Publishing, Inc.

Table of Contents

From the Authors 5

Foreword 7

Introduction 9

Using Textual Evidence
and Citations 9

How to Use This Book 12

Standards Correlations 13

Textual Evidence in Reading

Lesson 1: Introduction to Textual Evidence ... 16

Lesson 2: Citing with Direct Quotations 21

Lesson 3: Citing with Paraphrasing 24

Lesson 4: In-Text Citations with
Right-in-the-Text Answers 27

Lesson 5: In-Text Citations with
Inferential Answers 30

Reading Application Practice

Practice 1: Asking Questions 33

Practice 2: Identifying Key Details 37

Practice 3: Making Inferences 41

Practice 4: Finding the Moral
of the Story 45

Practice 5: Determining Figurative
Language 49

Practice 6: Analyzing Character 53

Practice 7: Determining Main Idea 57

Practice 8: Identifying Author's Purpose 61

Practice 9: Studying Text Structure 65

Practice 10: Comparing and Contrasting 69

Textual Evidence in Writing

Lesson 6: Gathering Sources 75

Lesson 7: Supporting a Claim 78

Lesson 8: Organizing Evidence 81

Lesson 9: Writing an Analysis 84

Lesson 10: Listing Sources 87

Writing Application Prompts

Prompt 1: Description Text Structure 90

Prompt 2: Sequence Text Structure 93

Prompt 3: Compare-and-Contrast
Text Structure 96

Prompt 4: Compare-and-Contrast
Text Structure 99

Prompt 5: Cause-and-Effect
Text Structure 102

Prompt 6: Description Text Structure 105

Prompt 7: Problem-and-Solution
Text Structure 108

Prompt 8: Chronological Text Structure 111

Prompt 9: Classification Text Structure 114

Prompt 10: Sequence Text Structure 117

Appendices

Appendix A: Answer Key 122

Appendix B: Additional Resources 126

Appendix C: Contents of the Digital
Resources 136

Appendix D: References Cited 136

From the Authors

Dedication

I dedicate this book to Deb Junkes for being my cheerleader in publication before I even knew I could play.—M.C.S.

I dedicate this book to Michael Schilling for always believing in me and giving me guidance and reassurance when I needed it most.—T.S

About Us

Terri Schilling, M.Ed., has a master's degree in educational leadership along with a reading specialist endorsement. She has been teaching for 15 years and presents at literacy professional development workshops.

Melissa Cheesman Smith, M.Ed., holds a master's degree in curriculum and instruction and has been teaching for 10 years. She teaches literacy classes for a university, presents at literacy conferences, and facilitates professional development workshops.

Acknowledgments

We would like to thank our editors and production team at Teacher Created Materials, namely Emily Smith and Stephanie Bernard, for taking our simple idea and crafting it into an easy-to-use resource for teachers. We'd also like to acknowledge Courtney Roberson for the beautiful cover and interior design of the book.

We'd like to thank Teacher Created Materials for believing that the teachers in the trenches are the root and heart of curriculum design, allowing resources to be produced from the ground up to create material that works for teachers to teach and students to learn.

From Melissa: I would like to thank my husband, David, and family for the extra time it took out of our family time to work on the book and for allowing me the time to develop trainings for teachers around the ideas based in this resource. I would especially like to thank my coauthor, Terri. As a friend and colleague, I have both love and respect for Terri as a friend and as a lifelong learner who inspires me to be a better teacher and push myself. "A friend is someone who knows all about you and still loves you."—Elbert Hubbard

From Terri: Thank you to Kete, Lisa, Dillon, and Autry for always bringing out the best in me; without all of you, I never could have followed my dreams. I am particularly appreciative to Melissa for asking me to partner with her in writing this book. It has been a rewarding experience following the process and learning from Melissa along the way. We have spent many years together growing as teachers and friends, of which I am truly grateful.

The Importance of Evidence

We live in a world where evidence is more important than ever. With people asserting all sorts of claims (i.e., "Believe me!", "No, believe me!", "No, don't believe either of those ding-dongs… BELIEVE ME!") in all sorts of formats (i.e., print, online, social media, television), the student who does not own the skill of cool, detached, reasoned, discernment is a student ill-prepared to face the demands of modern life.

Quite simply, the ability to understand and critically analyze evidence is the foremost key to avoid being duped (in a world filled with dupers). This is why I am such a fan of the Prove It! series. Melissa Cheesman Smith and Terri Schilling do not want students passively accepting assertions; they insist today's learners develop investigative eyes when it comes to analyzing contentions. Their work focuses on asking students to probe deeper, think critically, and get to the core of WHY a claim ought to be believed. Their work promotes meritocracy— the best ideas supported by the most convincing evidence wins. Forget the cult of personality. Throw away the unsupportable, inflammatory claims. Simply provide concrete, logical evidence to support your points, and the rest will take care of itself. In order to sustain a well-informed democracy, this is no small matter.

All in all, I love how this series rests on the foundation of knowing that reading requires students not to just form opinions about the text, but rather USE the text to form educated responses. That's a BIG WIN! From the embedded academic vocabulary instruction, to teaching students what credible and reliable sources are (so they can learn how to critically think and make informed decisions), to text structure and inferences, and on and on, there are many wonderful resources made available. And with such a well-organized progression of instruction, it's hard not to smile when you take a gander at all the goodies being offered.

As we all know, there is a sea change afoot in education. Evidence-based analysis is no longer something left for college-level instruction as students as young as seven years old are being asked to cite evidence to support their claims. To that end, materials that make weighty concepts accessible to young learners are essential. Do yourself a favor and allow expert educators to help connect the dots from assertions to evidence through a user-friendly set of instructional tools built specifically for the modern classroom. This Prove It! series rocks!

—Alan Lawrence Sitomer
California Teacher of the Year Award Winner
Author: *Mastering Short Response: Claim It! Cite It! Cement It!* by Scholastic

Using Textual Evidence and Citations

Instructionally, reading and writing change as they parallel the technological demands of the generation. Today, students must be able to write for purpose and with intent when conveying information on a topic, whether informational or argumentative, and they must be able to use printed text with an Internet technology base to back up that information. Providing purpose is essential for students because "sometimes our students' purposes don't match up with the purposes set for them to achieve in school" (Atkins 2011). We have to help set the purpose of success. To have purpose and intent, research on a topic is essential. The purpose of using text evidence is to teach students habits of argument. As Douglas Fisher and Nancy Frey point out, "students have to develop habits that allow them to mine texts for details, ideas, and deeper meanings" (2014, 4).

When finding evidence, students must learn how to cite textual evidence not only as a basic matter of research, but also as a way to validate their own statements and thinking through evidence-based arguments. When using textual evidence, a quotation or paraphrased text with an in-text citation is essential. While students may not need to formally conform to one specific style (MLA *or* APA), a basic in-text citation is required when quoting or paraphrasing text. This book will introduce students to best practices in citation formatting that can be used throughout elementary and middle school until they are required to learn certain styles in high school and college. For our purposes, MLA style will be used, as elementary and middle school students are more likely to be engaged in using page numbers from a given text rather than finding their own research.

Using textual evidence and citations is imperative for advancing through college and career readiness standards and also for college itself. Students will need this skill most directly for high-stakes testing, as much of the literacy testing (both reading and writing) today revolves around text-based evidence or document-based questions (DBQs). There is a direct connection between reading and writing when using text evidence and students having the ability to analyze text. Research shows that having students write an extended analytical response supported with text evidence and explanation has a positive impact on reading comprehension (Graham and Hebert 2010). Students will be required to use this skill for authoring papers in high school, in college, and possibly in their careers.

Students must learn how to read critically in literary and informational texts, looking for central ideas to comprehend and research further. So much of what we, as adults, process and read each day falls under the writing genres of informational or argumentative. We have to be critical to take in the information, sort it, and use what is credible to make informed decisions and create educated opinions. Douglas Fisher and Nancy Frey note that "understanding the purpose of and how others use evidence, reading closely looking for evidence, and annotating and sourcing texts are important aspects students must learn if they are going to be proficient composers who integrate evidence and respond to complex tasks" (2014, 5).

Using Textual Evidence and Citations *(cont.)*

Writing Genres

Three commonly used nonfiction writing genres today are informational, persuasive, and argumentative. While persuasive and argumentative may at first seem synonymous, as they each state claims, give reasons, and provide evidence, the differences between the two are significant:

- **Persuasive writing** aims to prove a claim through opinion, often through an emotional appeal, followed by personal anecdotes and reasons that may be effective but do not completely verify the claim.

- **Argumentative writing** aims to prove a claim through a series of logical statements, followed by facts, examples, and evidence that is verifiable.

Educators must teach students a unique skill set to help write within these genres using technological demands now required to present information. These skills require students today to be able do the following skills.

Locate Resources

- Question what is found on the Internet, and filter through what is and is not related to the specific topic.

- Know not only how to locate information but how to determine what a credible and reliable source looks like. Know the reason behind why these sources are imperative to use when doing research.

- Understand how to find credible and reliable sources.

Gather Resources

- Use a variety of multimodal sources to thoroughly encompass the totality of the topic researched. Writing is now created in a multimodal fashion. This means that students are no longer simply looking up facts in encyclopedias and regurgitating the information in their own words. The main source of information today is the Internet. Within the Internet, there are videos, news reports, websites, and infographics that provide a variety of ways to research, organize, and write about various topics.

- Find enough evidence to support a solid understanding of the topic, allowing it to be reorganized in a way that will be presentable for the intended audience.

Select and Organize Evidence

- Interpret the text. Read to determine which evidence correlates to the specific reasons, intent, and purpose of the topic.

- Find short, purposeful sections of the text that relate directly to a topic, whether through information or reason.

Write with Purpose and Intent

- Show critical thinking by analyzing the resources found and using in-text citations.

- Cite using paraphrasing.

- Cite using exact quotations.

- Understand the definition and ramifications of plagiarism.

Using Textual Evidence and Citations *(cont.)*

In addition to understanding how to locate sources and gather reliable information, learning how to cite textual evidence is a key component in reading and writing education today.

Textual Evidence Vocabulary

Use text-evidence vocabulary (*citation vs. quotation*) when teaching. Helping students understand the vocabulary will support the content of the lessons and ensure student success in the activities. It may be helpful to review words and phrases specific to textual evidence before beginning the lessons. For easy reference, a text evidence vocabulary chart is included on page 126.

In-Text Citations in Reading

Students must learn how to read critically in literary and informational texts through close reading, looking for central ideas to comprehend and research further. Students must be aware that sometimes they "need to read because they will be asked to synthesize information or produce ideas based on evidence" (Fisher and Frey 2014, 2). Students have to be critical to take in information, sort it, and use what is credible to make informed decisions or to create educated opinions. In this product, students will practice such skills by reading pieces of informational text on similar topics. They will closely read and annotate the passages. They will also focus on specific skills within the close reading to enhance their annotation skills. Students will answer comprehension questions and cite textual evidence in their answers. A rubric for close-reading annotations is provided on page 129.

In-Text Citations in Writing

It is critical for students to learn to write using more than their opinions as support. Students should also learn to determine their intended audience as well as decide on the purpose of their writing, because we "organize events, ideas, and arguments in a coherent fashion for a purpose and to meet the needs of an audience" (Fisher and Frey 2014, 10). Students must learn to find relevant and credible sources, decipher what information is relevant to their topic, and use evidence from the text to support their explanations. In this resource, the reading passages are designed to be informational while the writing passages are designed to be argumentative, so students can logically use textual evidence in their writing. Students will be prompted to cite textual evidence to support their responses. A rubric for citing textual evidence in writing is provided on page 130.

How to Use This Book

It is imperative that students receive direct instruction on all the elements for using textual evidence. This resource includes everything needed for students to learn basic textual evidence skills in reading and writing. There are four main sections of the book for students to practice all facets of using textual evidence in reading and writing.

Textual Evidence in Reading

Students will answer comprehension questions based on narrative, informative, or argumentative texts. They will paraphrase and use direct quotations, and then cite these resources to support their claims.

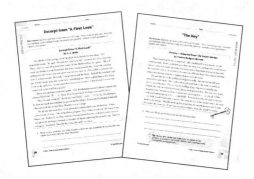

Reading Application Practice

Students will practice close reading passages using annotation strategies, answer questions related to the texts, and practically apply textual evidence with skills learned in the reading lessons.

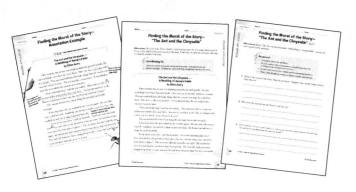

Textual Evidence in Writing

Students will practice gathering and organizing sources and supporting claims with evidence found in the text.

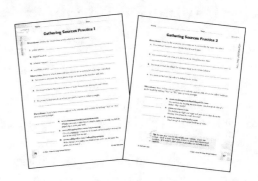

Writing Application Prompts

Students will read passages and will be given writing prompts. If directed by the teacher, they can then use the Internet to research the topics further and find additional evidence related to the prompts. Students are asked to use basic writing organization practices of including an introduction, body content, and a conclusion for each written response. Within the prompts, students practically apply their textual evidence skills learned in the lessons to complete the prompt.

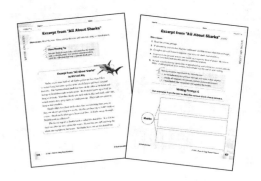

Standards Correlations

Shell Education is committed to producing educational materials that are research and standards based. In this effort, all products are correlated to the academic standards of all 50 United States, the District of Columbia, the Department of Defense Dependent Schools, and all Canadian provinces.

How to Find Standards Correlations

The general standards are provided in the Digital Resources (standards.pdf). Or, to print a customized correlation report of this product for your state, visit our website at **www.tcmpub. com/administrators/correlations** and follow the on-screen directions. If you require assistance in printing correlation reports, please contact Customer Service at 1-800-777-3450.

Purpose and Intent of Standards

The Every Student Succeeds Act (ESSA) mandates that all states adopt challenging academic standards that help students meet the goal of college and career readiness. While many states had already adopted academic standards prior to ESSA, the act continues to hold states accountable for detailed and comprehensive standards.

Standards are designed to focus instruction and guide adoption of curricula. Standards are statements that describe the criteria necessary for students to meet specific academic goals. They define the knowledge, skills, and content students should acquire at each level. Standards are also used to develop standardized tests to evaluate students' academic progress.

Teachers are required to demonstrate how their lessons meet state standards. State standards are used in development of all of our products, so educators can be assured they meet the academic requirements of each state.

College and Career Readiness Standards

Today's College and Career Readiness (CCR) standards offer guidelines for preparing K–12 students with the knowledge and skills that are necessary to succeed in postsecondary job training and education. CCR standards include the Common Core State Standards (CCSS) as well as other state-adopted standards such as the Texas Essential Knowledge and Skills (TEKS) and the Virginia Standards of Learning (SOL). The CCR standards listed on page 14 support the objectives presented throughout the lessons.

McREL Compendium

Each year, McREL analyzes state standards and revises the compendium to produce a general compilation of national standards. The standards listed on page 14 support the objectives presented throughout the lessons.

TESOL and WIDA Standards

The lessons in this book promote English language development for English language learners.

ISTE Standards

The International Society for Technology in Education (ISTE) standards provide guidelines for the knowledge and skills needed to succeed in the twenty-first century.

Standards Correlations *(cont.)*

Literacy Standards

3rd Grade	**Reading**	• Ask and answer questions to demonstrate understanding of a text, referring explicitly to the text as the basis for the answers.
	Writing	• With guidance and support from adults, use technology to produce and publish writing (using keyboarding skills) as well as to interact and collaborate with others. • Conduct short research projects that build knowledge about a topic. • Recall information from experiences or gather information from print and digital sources; take brief notes on sources and sort evidence into provided categories.
4th Grade	**Reading**	• Quote accurately from a text when explaining what the text says explicitly and when drawing inferences from the text.
	Writing	• With some guidance and support from adults, use technology, including the Internet, to produce and publish writing as well as to interact and collaborate with others. • Conduct short research projects that use several sources to build knowledge through investigation of different aspects of a topic. • Recall relevant information from experiences or gather relevant information from print and digital sources; take notes and categorize information; and provide a list of sources. • Draw evidence from literary or informational texts to support analysis, reflection, and research.
5th Grade	**Reading**	• Quote accurately from a text when explaining what the text says explicitly and when drawing inferences from the text.
	Writing	• With some guidance and support from adults, use technology, including the Internet, to produce and publish writing as well as to interact and collaborate with others. • Conduct short research projects that use several sources to build knowledge through investigation of different aspects of a topic. Recall relevant information from experiences or gather relevant information from print and digital sources; summarize or paraphrase information in notes and finished work; and provide a list of sources. • Draw evidence from literary or informational texts to support analysis, reflection, and research.

Reading Lessons and Application

Textual Evidence in Reading

Lesson 1: Introduction to Textual Evidence..16

Lesson 2: Citing with Direct Quotations..21

Lesson 3: Citing with Paraphrasing...24

Lesson 4: In-Text Citations with Right-in-the-Text Answers................27

Lesson 5: In-Text Citations with Inferential Answers 30

Reading Application Practice

Practice 1: Asking Questions...33

Practice 2: Identifying Key Details..37

Practice 3: Making Inferences...41

Practice 4: Finding the Moral of the Story 45

Practice 5: Determining Figurative Language 49

Practice 6: Analyzing Character 53

Practice 7: Determining Main Idea 57

Practice 8: Identifying Author's Purpose..61

Practice 9: Studying Text Structure 65

Practice 10: Comparing and Contrasting 69

Introduction to Textual Evidence

🔍 Objective

Students will learn the definitions and uses of textual evidence, quotations, and paraphrasing in academic writing.

✏️ Materials

- copies of *Matching* (page 17; page17.pdf)
- copies of *"Soccer"* (page 18; page18.pdf)
- copies of *True/False* (page 19; page19.pdf)
- copies of *"Giraffes"* (page 20; page20.pdf)
- highlighters

💡 Essential Question

How do I use textual evidence to answer questions in reading?

Guided Practice

1. Begin by explaining to students the purpose of textual evidence. Tell students, "When we read or write, we often use parts of the text to give answers or to help form opinions and prove points. When we do this, we use what is called *textual evidence*. This means we use exact words (also called quotations) or general ideas (known as paraphrasing) from the text to support the points we are explaining or arguing and then include in-text citations."

2. Tell students, "When you use someone else's ideas, you have to cite the text. This means you must give credit to the author who originally wrote the text. If you don't, this can be considered plagiarism. Plagiarism is taking someone else's words or thoughts and passing them off as your own. You do not need to cite something if the idea is your own or is common knowledge, but you do need to cite if you got the idea or words from another source."

3. Distribute *Matching* and *"Soccer"* (pages 17–18), and work with students to match the vocabulary words to the definitions. Then, read the passage together, and have students choose parts of the text that would be good support for their answers to the reading comprehension question. Finally, help students determine which part of the text would be strong support to prove their point for the prompt.

Independent Practice

- Have students complete *True/False* and *"Giraffes"* (pages 19–20) in class, as homework, or as an assessment to ensure they can complete the skill independently.

Additional Support

Have students annotate each individual sentence, indicating which text relates to each question.

Matching

Directions: Match the words about citing sources to their definitions.

_____ **1.** text

_____ **2.** in-text citation

_____ **3.** plagiarism

_____ **4.** direct quotation

_____ **5.** paraphrasing

a. stating the author and page number from a source when using a direct quotation or paraphrasing

b. restatement or rewording of an idea from a text

c. the exact words of someone else woven into your writing, noted by using quotation marks

d. the original piece of writing being cited

e. the practice of taking someone else's work and passing it off as your own

Directions: Answer the question.

1. Use your own words to describe what *plagiarism* means. What is an example of plagiarism that you have come across?

_____

_____

_____

_____

_____

GUIDED PRACTICE

Name _____ Date _____

"Soccer"

Directions: Read the passage. Then, answer the questions.

Soccer
by Melinda Ramos

Soccer is a sport played between two teams of 11 players each. It is the most popular sport in the world. In some countries, it is called football. Soccer is played on rectangular shaped grass or turf field called a pitch. There is a goal at each end of the pitch. The object of the game is to score the ball in the goal using only your feet. A goalkeeper may use his hands or arms to block the ball from going in the goal. Whichever team gets more goals, wins the game. The biggest and most famous international soccer competition is called the FIFA World Cup, and it happens every four years.

page 1

1. Underline the textual evidence that best answers the following question: *What is the object of the game?*

2. Highlight the textual evidence that would be best to use in a paper about soccer that explains what each player does.

True/False

Directions: Write *True* or *False* next to each statement about textual evidence.

_____ **1.** Textual evidence can be used to help answer questions in reading or to provide support to a writing topic.

_____ **2.** In-text citations are required every time you write.

_____ **3.** Paraphrasing means that you write someone else's idea in your own words, but you don't have to give them credit.

_____ **4.** Direct quotations are exact words used as support.

_____ **5.** An example of plagiarism would be copying two sentences that someone else wrote on the Internet and making it seem as if you were the one who wrote the words by not giving an in-text citation.

Directions: Rewrite the false sentences above so that they are true.

_____

_____

_____

_____

_____

_____

_____

"Giraffes"

Directions: Read the passage. Then, answer the questions.

Giraffes
by Maria Collin

The average height of a giraffe is around 16–18 feet (5–6 meters). Giraffes are the tallest land animals in the world. They have long legs, long necks, and spotted patterns. Giraffes live mostly in savanna areas in Africa. Their height allows them to eat leaves and shoots that are higher than other animals can reach. They especially love leaves from acacia trees. Their long tongues help them pull leaves from the trees. A giraffe spends most of the day eating and eats about 100 pounds (45.36 kilograms) of leaves and twigs a day.

page 1

1. Highlight the textual evidence that would be best to use in a paper about giraffes that describes their eating patterns.

2. Underline the textual evidence that best answers the following question: *Where do giraffes usually live?* Then, answer the question using the text you underlined to support your answer.

_____

_____

_____

_____

_____

Tip: Textual evidence should prove exactly what it is you are trying to say. The evidence should consist of carefully chosen words that match the question or topic.

INDEPENDENT PRACTICE

Citing with Direct Quotations

Objective

Students will find and use direct quotations and correctly cite them.

Materials

- copies of *"Take to the Sky"* (page 22; page22.pdf)
- copies of *"Underwater Architect"* (page 23; page23.pdf)
- highlighters

Essential Question

How do I find a direct quotation related to a question and correctly cite it?

Guided Practice

1. Begin by explaining to students that when proving a point based on an idea in the text, using the exact words from the text as support helps to "prove" the point. Tell students there is a way to write so the reader knows when words are used from an outside source.

2. Distribute *"Take to the Sky"* (page 22). Read aloud the excerpt, and have students follow along. After reading, ask students, "What is the difference between hang gliding and parasailing?" Give students time to locate and highlight the answer.

3. Once students have found the sentence(s) that prove the answer, they should formulate their written responses. Remind students that they must put exact text inside quotation marks. Tell students that they don't have to quote an entire sentence; they can pick only the key words that best provide the answer.

4. Show students how to create in-text citations or parenthetical references. Write several examples on the board following MLA format, such as (Shale 1), (Roberts 24), (Jackson par. 3), or (McDonald par. 7). For more information, see *MLA Citing Source Reference* on page 131.

5. Have students practice with the second question, "Why was zip-lining first created?" Guide students in answering with a direct quotation and a citation. Redirect as needed to be sure formatting of the citation is correct. Students may choose to share their answers with the class.

Independent Practice

- Have students complete *"Underwater Architect"* (page 23) in class, as homework, or as an assessment to ensure they can complete the skill independently.

Additional Support

Have students circle or highlight the words in the text, so they correctly quote the passage.

Name _____ Date _____

"Take to the Sky"

Directions: Answer each question using a direct quotation and an in-text citation.

Take to the Sky
by Jeff Shale

Have you ever wanted to feel as free as a bird? People have dreamed of flying for thousands of years. For many, the invention of airplanes was a dream come true. Since then, dreamers have found several other ways to feel as though they were flying.

Parasailing is one way people can experience the feeling of soaring like a kite. A parasailer wears a parachute and sits on a boat. The boat drives quickly through the water. The parachute catches the breeze. And then, liftoff! Hang gliding is similar to parasailing. The difference is that hang gliding is done over land and not over water. Hang gliders don't rely on boats to pull them. They jump off cliffs to achieve liftoff.

Zip-lining is another way to fly. People needed a way to quickly get from one place to another, so zip-lining was created. People strung a thick cable between two tall peaks. Then, they tied a cable around themselves. They could use the cable to zip back and forth. Today, you can zip-line for sport. You can even zip-line across an entire mountain range!

For those who dream of taking to the sky, there are many ways to explore the art of flying—if you dare!

page 1

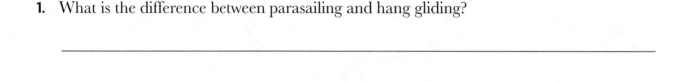

1. What is the difference between parasailing and hang gliding?

_____

_____

2. Why was zip-lining first created?

_____

_____

"Underwater Architect"

Directions: Answer each question using a direct quotation and in-text citation.

Underwater Architect
by Beatrice Shell

The chambered nautilus is related to the octopus and squid. Like its relatives, it has a lot of arms—up to 90! But the nautilus has something the others don't have. It has a beautiful shell that protects it from predators. The shell offers camouflage. The top of the shell is dark. It blends in with the dark sea. It is light on the bottom. This blends in with the light coming from above the water. The shell is divided inside. New rooms, or chambers, are added to the shell as the animal grows.

The nautilus can pull itself inside the shell if it feels threatened. Its hard shell offers protection from the sharp teeth of predators. Snails and hermit crabs also use shells for protection. In this same way, humans once built walls around castles. These tall rock walls protected the people inside the castle from arrows and cannons.

page 1

1. Why is the bottom of the nautilus shell lightly colored?

_____

_____

2. What other two animals besides the nautilus use shells for protection?

_____

_____

Tip: Be sure that you use quotation marks (" ") around the exact words used in your answer. Then, format the citation correctly (Author __).

Citing with Paraphrasing

Objective

Students will paraphrase a text and correctly cite it.

Materials

- copies of *Excerpt from "The Story of Doctor Dolittle"* (page 25; page25.pdf)
- copies of *Excerpt from "Playing for Keeps"* (page 26; page26.pdf)
- highlighters

Essential Question

How do I find text related to a question and correctly paraphrase and cite it?

Guided Practice

1. Explain to students that sometimes exact quotations are not needed, but instead, general ideas can be paraphrased. Explain that to paraphrase means to talk about parts of the text in one's own words. However, a citation should still be given to credit the author of the original text.

2. Distribute *Excerpt from "The Story of Doctor Dolittle"* (page 25). Read the passage aloud as students follow along. After reading, ask students to think about the first question. Give students time to locate, highlight, and share examples.

3. Once students have found the sentence(s) that support their answers, tell students to paraphrase the information from the text and include citations. Help them understand how to summarize their chosen sentences in their own words. Write an example of an MLA citation on the board: *(Lofting 1).* Guide students in formulating their responses using paraphrasing and creating the correct citation.

4. Have students answer the second question. Remind them that they should not include quotation marks when paraphrasing. Redirect as needed to be sure formatting of the citation is correct. Students may choose to share their answers with the class.

Independent Practice

- Have students complete *Excerpt from "Playing for Keeps"* (page 26) in class, as homework, or as an assessment to ensure they can complete the skill independently.

Additional Support

Remind students of the differences between a direct quotation and paraphrasing.

Excerpt from "The Story of Doctor Dolittle"

Directions: On a separate sheet of paper, answer the questions by paraphrasing and using in-text citations.

Excerpt from "The Story of Doctor Dolittle"
by Hugh Lofting

That winter was a very blustery one. One evening in December, all of the animals were sitting 'round the cozy fire in the kitchen. The Doctor was reading aloud to them out of books he had written himself in animal language. Suddenly, the owl, Too-Too, said, "Sh! What's that noise outside?"

They all listened, and presently they heard the sound of someone running. Then, the door flew open, and the monkey, Chee-Chee, sprinted in, terribly out of breath.

"Doctor!" he cried, "I've just received a message from a cousin of mine in Africa. There is a terrible epidemic among the monkeys out there. They are all catching it—and they are perishing in hundreds. They have heard of you, and beg you to travel to Africa to eradicate the sickness."

"Who delivered the message?" asked the Doctor.

"A swallow," said Chee-Chee, "and she is outside on the rain barrel."

"Quickly, bring her by the fire," instructed the Doctor. "She must be quivering with the cold. The swallows flew south six weeks ago!"

So the swallow was brought in, all huddled and shivering; and although she was a little frightened at the beginning, she soon warmed up. Delicately perched on the edge of the mantelpiece, she began to converse.

page 1

1. How do you know this could not be a true story?

2. How do you know the Doctor likes animals?

Name _____ Date _____

Excerpt from "Playing for Keeps"

Directions: On a separate sheet of paper, answer the questions by paraphrasing and using in-text citations.

Excerpt from "Playing for Keeps"
by Carmen Board

My dad loves playing board games—dusty, old, boring board games. At least once a week, he makes the whole family play together. It's totally unfair! There are other things we could be doing, but we just sit and play the same stupid games.

At school, my friend Jackson has every video game ever made. His parents let him play them in his room at night before he goes to bed.

"You're totally lucky," I tell him. "My parents only let me play digi stuff for a little while, and then my dad puts it all away so we can play games together."

"Your dad plays games with you?" Jackson asks.

"Not video games. My family plays board games." I do not say it nicely.

"Wow, man! That's awesome. I pretty much never see my dad. I would love to play something with him. That would rock."

I never thought about it that way before. I thought my dad was totally boring, but maybe he just wants our family to spend time together.

"Want to come over and play Sharks Versus Snails?" Jackson asks.

"I actually kind of feel like playing a board game right now," I say.

"Yeah, me too. Can I come with you?"

"Totally!"

page 1

---

1. Why is the narrator jealous of Jackson?

2. Why do the boys decide not to play video games at the end?

Tip: You don't need quotation marks when paraphrasing. You can restate the general idea of the answer by using your own words. Then, complete your answer with an in-text citation.

In-Text Citations with Right-in-the-Text Answers

🔍 Objective

Students will use in-text citations to answer questions with answers directly stated in the text.

✏️ Materials

- copies of *Excerpt from "The Time Machine"* (page 28; page28.pdf)
- copies of *"The Key"* (page 29; page29.pdf)
- pens or pencils
- highlighters

💡 Essential Question

How do I use text to help answer a question?

Guided Practice

1. Remind students that exact excerpts from a text can be used as evidence to support an answer and that they require quotation marks and citations.

2. Distribute *Excerpt from "The Time Machine"* (page 28). Have students read the question, so they know what information to look for. Then, read the passage aloud. As you read, model think-aloud strategies for students. Have students annotate and highlight text that will support their answers.

3. Have students orally suggest parts of the text that directly relate to the question being asked. Explain that sometimes answers to questions will be in the text, and sometimes they will have to be inferred. In this case, the answer comes directly from the text.

4. Guide students on how to develop their answers to the question. (For this question, the answer can be found at the end of the third paragraph.) Explain to students that as a general pattern, questions are best answered in three sentences: the first sentence answers the question, the second sentence provides support through a text citation using a text evidence starter, and the third sentence explains or connects by summarizing the answer. Use the text evidence starters on pages 127–128 to aid students in choosing an appropriate starter to introduce their text evidence.

5. Remind students that a citation is needed directly following a quotation. In this case, the abbreviation *par.* is used to reference a specific paragraph.

Independent Practice

- Have students complete *"The Key"* (page 29) in class, as homework, or as an assessment to ensure they can complete the skill independently.

Additional Support

Students can write the author's last name and page number in the margin next to the quotation to easily identify the in-text citation when needed.

Name _____ Date _____

Excerpt from "The Time Machine"

Directions: Read the question at the bottom of the page. Then, read the passage. Annotate and highlight while reading to help you answer the question. Include a cited quotation to support your answer.

Excerpt from "The Time Machine"
by H. G. Wells

The Medical Man got up out of his chair and peered into the thing. "It's beautifully made," he said. "It took two years to make," retorted the Time Traveller. Then, when we had all imitated the action of the Medical Man, he spoke. "Now I want you clearly to understand that this lever, being pressed over, sends the machine gliding into the future, and this other reverses the motion. This saddle represents the seat of a time traveller. Presently, I am going to pull the lever. And off the machine will go. It will vanish, pass into future time, and disappear. Have a good look at the thing. Look at the table, too. Satisfy yourselves there is no trickery. I don't want to waste this model only to be told I'm a quack."

There was perhaps a minute's pause. The Psychologist seemed about to speak but changed his mind. Then the Time Traveller put forth his finger toward the lever.

"No," he said suddenly. "Lend me your hand." And turning to the Psychologist, he took his hand and told him to put out his forefinger. It was the Psychologist himself who sent forth the model Time Machine on its voyage.

We all saw the lever turn. I am absolutely certain there was no trickery. There was a breath of wind. The lamp flame jumped. One of the candles on the mantel was blown out. Suddenly, the little machine swung round, became indistinct, and was seen as a ghost for perhaps a second, as an eddy of faintly glittering brass and ivory. Then it was gone. Vanished! Save for the lamp, the table was bare.

1. While at first we believe the Time Traveller will be the one to pull the lever, whom does the author have send forth the Time Machine?

_____

_____

"The Key"

Directions: Read the question at the bottom of the page. Then, read the passage. Annotate and highlight while reading to help you answer the question. Include a cited quotation to support your answer.

The Key—Adapted from *The Secret Garden* by Frances Hodgson Burnett

Mary looked at the key a long time. She wondered if it was the key to the closed garden. If she could find out where the door was, perhaps she could open it and see what was inside the walls. It was because it had been shut up so long that she wanted to see it. It seemed as if it must be different from other places and that something strange must have happened there over the years.

She put the key in her pocket and began to walk. No one but herself ever seemed to come there. She could walk slowly and look at the wall, or rather at the ivy growing on it. The ivy was the baffling thing. However carefully she looked, she only saw thickly growing, glossy, dark-green leaves. She was very much disappointed. Something of her contrariness came back to her as she paced the walk and looked over it at the treetops inside. It seemed so silly, she said to herself, to be near it and not be able to get in. She took the key in her pocket when she went back to the house. And she made up her mind that she would always carry it with her when she went out. If she ever found the hidden door, she would be ready.

1. Why can't Mary use the key to get into the closed garden?

_____

_____

_____

Tip: Be sure your answer has three parts: an answer to the question, a quotation and in-text citation, and a summary with a connection or explanation.

In-Text Citations with Inferential Answers

Objective

Students will answer questions by citing text to prove their inferences about a text.

Materials

- copies of *"How Are Fossil Fuels Made?"* (page 31; page31.pdf)
- copies of *"It's the Law! But Why?"* (page 32; page32.pdf)
- highlighters

Essential Question

How do I use a quotation to help support my inference?

Additional Support

Guide students to focus on using only one quotation and one simple explanation in each answer.

Guided Practice

1. Tell students, "When you are answering questions about a text, you should read the text, looking for evidence to support your answer, and then quote and cite the text." Explain to students that sometimes there are clues provided in the text, but the text might not state an answer exactly. When that happens, they will have to make inferences.

2. Distribute *"How Are Fossil Fuels Made?"* (page 31). Have students read the question first so they know what information to look for as they annotate. Read the passage aloud. Model think-aloud strategies for students as you read. Have students annotate and highlight the text that will best support their answers.

3. Have students answer the question. Explain to students how to select pieces of the text that will help them develop their answers. Point out that one part of the text discusses bodies of plants and animals on the ocean floor. Though it does not give the answer directly, it can be inferred that something that happened so long ago cannot be recreated.

4. Explain that the next step for each student is to write an explanation in one's own words using quotations and a text evidence starter to support the answer. Use the text evidence starters on pages 127–128 to aid students in choosing a starter to introduce their text evidence. Remind students that direct text must be in quotation marks and cited properly. Use *Quotation Mark Rules* (page 134) to discuss the grammatical rules when writing with quotation marks. Remind students that a citation is needed directly following a quotation. In this case, the abbreviation *par.* is used to reference a specific paragraph.

5. Have students find additional quotations to strengthen their answers. Check students' work to be sure the quotations they've chosen support their inferences and are properly cited and punctuated.

Independent Practice

- Have students independently complete *"It's the Law! But Why?"* (page 32) in class, as homework, or as an assessment to ensure they can complete the skill.

"How Are Fossil Fuels Made?"

Directions: Read the question at the bottom of the page. Then, read the passage. Annotate and highlight while reading to help you answer the question. On a separate sheet of paper, include two cited quotations to support your answer.

How Are Fossil Fuels Made?
by Andrew Roberts

Petroleum and natural gas are made from plants and animals that died hundreds of millions of years ago. Back then, very small plants and animals floated in the oceans. They were much like the ones we know now. The plants were called phytoplankton. They were able to use photosynthesis just like other plants. The animals were called zooplankton. They ate other tiny animals. They also ate living and dead plants. Though tiny, there were billions of them in the oceans. Because they were living, their bodies held lots of the sun's energy. They also held energy from food they ate.

As they died, their bodies settled on the ocean floor. They piled up for millions of years. The piles got thicker over time. They got mixed and buried by sediments. The layers of sediments and dead things made pressure. They also made things very hot.

Pressure and heat transformed the buried plants and animals. They were no longer solids, but materials that could flow. In time, they became petroleum and natural gas. Movements in the earth pushed them closer to the surface.

Coal was made in a similar way but on land. Millions of years ago, there were swamps over large parts of Earth's surface. Lots of plants and animals lived there. As these organisms died, their bodies piled up on the ground. Years and years went by. More materials piled up thicker and thicker. Everything got buried deep underground. This created a hot, high-pressure environment. And that changed the materials into coal and natural gas.

1. Is it possible to recreate fossil fuels to use today, so we never run out of them?

"It's the Law! But Why?"

Directions: Read the question at the bottom of the page. Then, read the passage. Annotate and highlight while reading to help you answer the question. Include at least two cited quotations to support your answer.

It's the Law! But Why?
by Devin Garrison

Laws keep people safe. They help us live together peacefully. But sometimes, there are laws that don't make any sense at all.

In Alabama, you can't wear a fake mustache in church. It's against the law to sing off key in North Carolina. And don't take a lion to the movies. It's against the law in Maryland. In Kansas, you could be in trouble for singing at night. In Ohio, it's illegal to dye chickens. You could be arrested if you ride a camel in Nevada. And you can't eat ice cream on Sunday in Oregon. You are breaking the law if you do. Who knew?

It's almost always a good idea to obey the law. But even police officers ignore the kookiest laws. If there's a thief on the loose, a fake moustache isn't such a big deal! Some of these laws are very old. So it's hard to know why they were ever written. But we can't ignore every law. Laws are only powerful if we obey them. What will you do the next time you find a strange law?

1. Should outdated laws be removed?

_____

_____

_____

_____

Tip: Remember to add a final thought in your own words. Do not end your answer with a quotation.

51700—Prove It! Using Textual Evidence

Asking Questions

Materials

- *Asking Questions—Annotation Example* (page 34; page34.pdf) (optional)

- copies of *Asking Questions—"Man's Best Friend"* (pages 35–36; page35.pdf)

- colored pencils

Procedure

1. Distribute *Asking Questions—"Man's Best Friend"* (pages 35–36). Have students read the passage independently.

2. Have students reread the passage, this time completing a close reading and annotation of the text using colored pencils. Students should focus specifically on the close-reading skill of asking questions.

   - *Asking Questions—Annotation Example* (page 34) can be used for your reference, to model annotating for students, or as an individual scaffold for students as necessary.

Close-Reading Skill—Asking Questions

Have students read the questions prior to rereading the story. Using colored pencils, have students annotate the text as they read by writing questions they have.

3. Assign the text-dependent questions on page 36. Explain to students that their responses should accurately answer the questions, provide evidence (direct quotations or paraphrasing) from the reading passage to support answers, include in-text citations, and conclude with final thoughts that connect or further explain the answers.

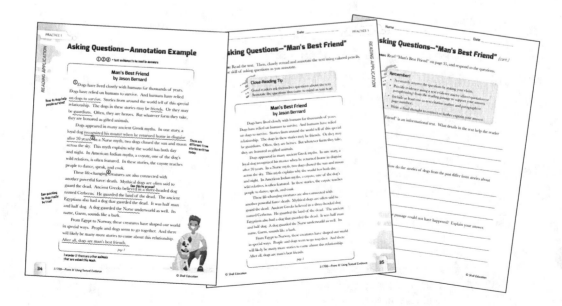

Asking Questions—Annotation Example

①②③ = text evidence to be used in answers

Man's Best Friend
by Jason Bernard

①Dogs have lived closely with humans for thousands of years. Dogs have relied on humans to survive. And humans have relied on dogs to survive. Stories from around the world tell of this special relationship. The dogs in these stories may be friends. Or they may be guardians. Often, they are heroes. But whatever form they take, they are honored as gifted animals.

How do dogs help people survive?

Dogs appeared in many ancient Greek myths. In one story, a loyal dog recognized his master when he returned home in disguise after 20 years. ②In a Norse myth, two dogs chased the sun and moon across the sky. This myth explains why the world has both day and night. In American Indian myths, a coyote, one of the dog's wild relatives, is often featured. In these stories, the coyote teaches people to dance, speak, and cook.

These are different from stories written today.

These life-changing ③creatures are also connected with another powerful force: death. Mythical dogs are often said to guard the dead. Ancient Greeks believed in a three-headed dog named Cerberus. He guarded the land of the dead. The ancient Egyptians also had a dog that guarded the dead. It was half man and half dog. A dog guarded the Norse underworld as well. Its name, Garm, sounds like a bark.

Can this be proven?

Can guarding by dogs really be true?

From Egypt to Norway, these creatures have shaped our world in special ways. People and dogs seem to go together. And there will likely be many more stories to come about this relationship. After all, dogs are man's best friends.

page 1

I wonder if there are other animals that are valued this much.

Asking Questions—"Man's Best Friend"

Directions: Read the text. Then, closely reread and annotate the text using colored pencils. Focus on the skill of asking questions as you annotate.

Close-Reading Tip

Good readers ask themselves questions about the text. Annotate the questions that come to mind as you read.

Man's Best Friend
by Jason Bernard

Dogs have lived closely with humans for thousands of years. Dogs have relied on humans to survive. And humans have relied on dogs to survive. Stories from around the world tell of this special relationship. The dogs in these stories may be friends. Or they may be guardians. Often, they are heroes. But whatever form they take, they are honored as gifted animals.

Dogs appeared in many ancient Greek myths. In one story, a loyal dog recognized his master when he returned home in disguise after 20 years. In a Norse myth, two dogs chased the sun and moon across the sky. This myth explains why the world has both day and night. In American Indian myths, a coyote, one of the dog's wild relatives, is often featured. In these stories, the coyote teaches people to dance, speak, and cook.

These life-changing creatures are also connected with another powerful force: death. Mythical dogs are often said to guard the dead. Ancient Greeks believed in a three-headed dog named Cerberus. He guarded the land of the dead. The ancient Egyptians also had a dog that guarded the dead. It was half man and half dog. A dog guarded the Norse underworld as well. Its name, Garm, sounds like a bark.

From Egypt to Norway, these creatures have shaped our world in special ways. People and dogs seem to go together. And there will likely be many more stories to come about this relationship. After all, dogs are man's best friends.

page 1

Asking Questions—"Man's Best Friend" *(cont.)*

Directions: Read "Man's Best Friend" on page 35, and respond to the questions.

Remember!

- Accurately answer the questions by stating your claim.
- Provide evidence using a text evidence starter (direct quotation or paraphrasing) from the reading passage to support your answer.
- Include at least one in-text citation (author and paragraph or page number).
- Write a final thought to connect or further explain your answer.

1. "Man's Best Friend" is an informational text. What details in the text help the reader know this?

   _____

   _____

   _____

2. Based on this text, how do the stories of dogs from the past differ from stories about dogs today?

   _____

   _____

   _____

3. Which of the events in the passage could not have happened? Explain your answer.

   _____

   _____

   _____

Identifying Key Details

Materials

- *Identifying Key Details—Annotation Example* (page 38; page38.pdf) (optional)
- copies of *Identifying Key Details—"A Cry for Help"* (pages 39–40; page39.pdf)
- colored pencils

Procedure

1. Distribute *Identifying Key Details—"A Cry for Help"* (pages 39–40). Have students read the passage independently.

2. Have students reread the passage, this time completing a close reading and annotation of the text using colored pencils. Students should focus specifically on the close-reading skill of identifying key details.

   - *Identifying Key Details—Annotation Example* (page 38) can be used as reference, to model annotating for students, or as an individual scaffold for students as necessary.

   ### Close-Reading Skill—Identifying Key Details

   Have students use colored pencils to underline key details. Students should determine which key details are essential to understanding the text. Tell students if a detail can be left out of the passage without changing its meaning, it is not that important.

3. Assign the text-dependent questions on page 40. Explain to students that their responses should accurately answer the questions, provide evidence (direct quotations or paraphrasing) from the reading passage to support the answers, include in-text citations, and conclude with final thoughts that connect or further explain the answers.

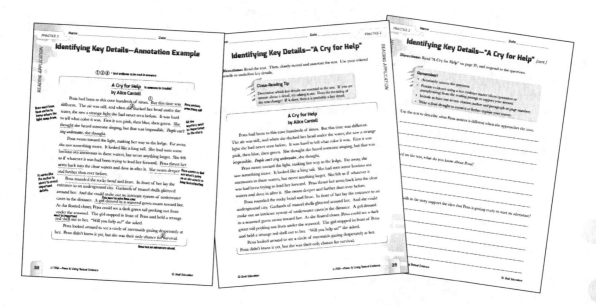

Identifying Key Details—Annotation Example

①②③ = text evidence to be used in answers

A Cry for Help   Is someone in trouble?
by Alice Cantell

①

Pena had been to this cove hundreds of times. But this time was   *Pena notices something odd.*

②

different. The air was still, and when she ducked her head under the

water, she saw a strange light she had never seen before. It was hard

to tell what color it was. First it was pink, then blue, then green. She   *All the mystery must be importatnt to the story.*

Pena must have been curious to know where the light came from.

thought she heard someone singing, but that was impossible. *People can't*

sing underwater, she thought.

Pena swam toward the light, making her way to the ledge. Far away,

she saw something move. It looked like a long tail. She had seen some

luscious sea anemones in these waters, but never anything larger. She felt

as if whatever it was had been trying to lead her forward. Pena thrust her

arms back into the clear waters and dove in after it. She swam deeper   *Pena wants to find out what's going on so she wants to keep investigating.*

and farther than ever before.

It seems like the author is about to reveal important details.

Pena rounded the rocky bend and froze. In front of her lay the

entrance to an underground city. Garlands of mussel shells glittered

around her. And she could make out an intricate system of underwater

This must be who Pena saw.

caves in the distance. A girl dressed in a seaweed gown swam toward her.

As she floated closer, Pena could see a dark green tail peeking out from

under the seaweed. The girl stopped in front of Pena and held a strange

must be important

red shell out to her. "Will you help us?" she asked.

Pena looked around to see a circle of mermaids gazing desperately at

③

her. Pena didn't know it yet, but she was their only chance for survival.

page 1   **Pena has an adventure ahead.**

Identifying Key Details—"A Cry for Help"

Directions: Read the text. Then, closely reread and annotate the text. Use your colored pencils to underline key details.

Close-Reading Tip

Determine which key details are essential to the text. If you are unsure about a detail, try taking it out. Does the meaning of the text change? If it does, then it is probably a key detail.

A Cry for Help
by Alice Cantell

Pena had been to this cove hundreds of times. But this time was different. The air was still, and when she ducked her head under the water, she saw a strange light she had never seen before. It was hard to tell what color it was. First it was pink, then blue, then green. She thought she heard someone singing, but that was impossible. *People can't sing underwater*, she thought.

Pena swam toward the light, making her way to the ledge. Far away, she saw something move. It looked like a long tail. She had seen some luscious sea anemones in these waters, but never anything larger. She felt as if whatever it was had been trying to lead her forward. Pena thrust her arms back into the clear waters and dove in after it. She swam deeper and farther than ever before.

Pena rounded the rocky bend and froze. In front of her lay the entrance to an underground city. Garlands of mussel shells glittered around her. And she could make out an intricate system of underwater caves in the distance. A girl dressed in a seaweed gown swam toward her. As she floated closer, Pena could see a dark green tail peeking out from under the seaweed. The girl stopped in front of Pena and held a strange red shell out to her. "Will you help us?" she asked.

Pena looked around to see a circle of mermaids gazing desperately at her. Pena didn't know it yet, but she was their only chance for survival.

page 1

Identifying Key Details—"A Cry for Help" *(cont.)*

Directions: Read "A Cry for Help" on page 39, and respond to the questions.

Remember!

- Accurately answer the questions by stating your claim.
- Provide evidence using a text evidence starter (direct quotation or paraphrasing) from the reading passage to support your answer.
- Include at least one in-text citation (author and paragraph or page number).
- Write a final thought to connect or further explain your answer.

1. Use the text to describe what Pena notices is different when she approaches the cove.

   _____

   _____

   _____

2. Based on the text, what do you know about Pena?

   _____

   _____

   _____

3. What details in the story support the idea that Pena is getting ready to start an adventure?

   _____

   _____

   _____

   _____

Making Inferences

Materials

- *Making Inferences—Annotation Example* (page 42; page42.pdf) (optional)
- copies of *Making Inferences— "From 613 King Street to Room 4F"* (pages 43–44; page43.pdf)
- colored pencils

Procedure

1. Distribute *Making Inferences—"From 613 King Street to Room 4F"* (pages 43–44). Have students read the passage independently.

2. Have students reread and complete a close reading and annotation of the text using colored pencils. Students should focus specifically on the close-reading skill of making inferences.

   - *Making Inferences—Annotation Example* (page 42) can be used as reference, to model annotating for students, or as an individual scaffold for students as necessary.

Close-Reading Skill—Making Inferences

Explain to students that to infer is to "read between the lines." Inferences can be made by asking questions while reading. Sometimes the answer is found directly in the text. When it is not, readers need to infer to determine the answer. Asking questions allows the reader to analyze and think critically about the text.

3. Assign the text-dependent questions on page 44. Explain to students that their responses should accurately answer the questions, provide evidence (direct quotations or paraphrasing) from the reading passage to support the answers, include in-text citations, and conclude with final thoughts that connect or further explain the answers.

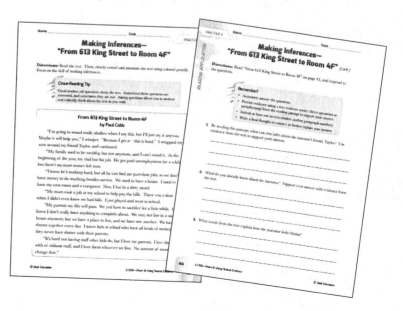

Making Inferences—Annotation Example

①②③ = text evidence to be used in answers

From 613 King Street to Room 4F
by Paul Cobb

"I'm going to sound really shallow when I say this, but I'll just say it anyway. Maybe it will help you," I whisper. ①("Because I get it—this is hard.") I wrapped my arm around my friend Taylor and continued.

③("My family used to be wealthy, but not anymore, and I can't stand it.) At the beginning of the year, my dad lost his job. He got paid unemployment for a while, but there's no more money left now.

The narrator sounds angry.

"I know he's working hard, but all he can find are part-time jobs, so we don't have money to do anything besides survive. (We used to have a house.) I used to have my own room and a computer. Now, I live in a dirty motel.

Because they were wealthy, it must have been a nice home.

"My mom took a job at my school to help pay the bills. There was a time when (I didn't even know we had bills.) I just played and went to school.

Lived a sheltered life.

Kids shouldn't have to worry about things like this.

"My parents say this will pass. We just have to sacrifice for a little while. I know I don't really have anything to complain about. We may not live in a nice house anymore, but we have a place to live, and we have one another. We have dinner together every day. I know kids at school who have all kinds of money, but they never have dinner with their parents.

②"It's hard not having stuff other kids do, but I love my parents. I love them with or without stuff, and I love them wherever we live. No amount of money can change that."

Feels sad/cares about parents

The narrator shows a character change from the way she used to be.

page 1

Making Inferences—
"From 613 King Street to Room 4F"

READING APPLICATION

Directions: Read the text. Then, closely reread and annotate the text using colored pencils. Focus on the skill of making inferences.

Close-Reading Tip

Good readers ask questions about the text. Sometimes these questions are answered, and sometimes they are not. Asking questions allows you to analyze and critically think about the text as you read.

From 613 King Street to Room 4F
by Paul Cobb

"I'm going to sound really shallow when I say this, but I'll just say it anyway. Maybe it will help you," I whisper. "Because I get it—this is hard." I wrapped my arm around my friend Taylor and continued.

"My family used to be wealthy, but not anymore, and I can't stand it. At the beginning of the year, my dad lost his job. He got paid unemployment for a while, but there's no more money left now.

"I know he's working hard, but all he can find are part-time jobs, so we don't have money to do anything besides survive. We used to have a house. I used to have my own room and a computer. Now, I live in a dirty motel.

"My mom took a job at my school to help pay the bills. There was a time when I didn't even know we had bills. I just played and went to school.

"My parents say this will pass. We just have to sacrifice for a little while. I know I don't really have anything to complain about. We may not live in a nice house anymore, but we have a place to live, and we have one another. We have dinner together every day. I know kids at school who have all kinds of money, but they never have dinner with their parents.

"It's hard not having stuff other kids do, but I love my parents. I love them with or without stuff, and I love them wherever we live. No amount of money can change that."

page 1

Making Inferences—
"From 613 King Street to Room 4F" *(cont.)*

Directions: Read "From 613 King Street to Room 4F" on page 43, and respond to the questions.

> ### Remember!
> - Accurately answer the questions by stating your claim.
> - Provide evidence using a text evidence starter (direct quotation or paraphrasing) from the reading passage to support your answer.
> - Include at least one in-text citation (author, paragraph number).
> - Write a final thought to connect or further explain your answer.

1. By reading this passage, what can you infer about the narrator's friend, Taylor? Use evidence from the text to support your answer.

   _____

   _____

   _____

2. What do you already know about the narrator? Support your answer with evidence from the text.

   _____

   _____

   _____

3. What words from the text explain how the narrator feels/thinks?

   _____

   _____

   _____

Finding the Moral of the Story

📝 Materials

- *Finding the Moral of the Story—Annotation Example* (page 46; page46.pdf) (optional)
- copies of *Finding the Moral of the Story—"The Ant and the Chrysalis"* (pages 47–48; page47.pdf)
- colored pencils

Procedure

1. Distribute *Finding the Moral of the Story—"The Ant and the Chrysalis"* (pages 47–48). Have students read the passage independently.

2. Have students reread and complete a close reading and annotation of the text, using colored pencils. Students should focus specifically on the close-reading skill of finding the moral of a story. Have students circle or underline the evidence in the text that helps them figure out the moral of the story.

   - *Finding the Moral of the Story—Annotation Example* (page 46) can be used as reference, to model annotating for students, or as an individual scaffold for students as necessary.

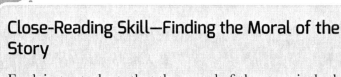

Close-Reading Skill—Finding the Moral of the Story

Explain to students that the moral of the story is the lesson that is learned. It often focuses on positive messages. Have students use colored pencils to underline words that help them identify the moral of the story.

3. Assign the text-dependent questions on page 48. Explain to students that their responses should accurately answer the questions, provide evidence (direct quotations or paraphrasing) from the reading passage to support the answers, include in-text citations, and conclude with final thoughts that connect or further explain the answers.

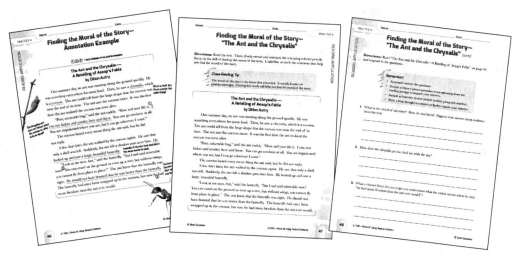

READING APPLICATION

Finding the Moral of the Story—
Annotation Example

①②③ = text evidence to be used in answers

The Ant and the Chrysalis—
A Retelling of Aesop's Fable
by Dillon Autry

One summer day, an ant was running along the ground quickly. He was searching everywhere for some food. Then, he saw a chrysalis, which is a cocoon. The ant could tell from the large shape that the cocoon was near the end of its time. The ant saw the cocoon move. It was the first time the ant realized the cocoon was even alive.

What is this? Are these exactly the same thing?

"Poor, miserable bug," said the ant rudely. "How sad your life is. ① I can run hither and yonder, here and there. You can go nowhere at all. You are imprisoned where you are, but I can go wherever I want."

The bragging ant does not know what the cocoon is— why is he so mean?

The cocoon heard every mean thing the ant said, but he did not reply.

A few days later, the ant walked by the cocoon again. He saw that only a shell was left. Suddenly, the ant felt a shadow pass over him. He looked up and saw a large, beautiful butterfly.

I wonder if the ant feels bad about the mean words he used.

"Look at me now, Ant," said the butterfly. "Am I sad and miserable now? ② You can crawl on the ground or even up a tree, but without wings, you cannot fly from place to place." The ant knew that the butterfly was right. He should not have boasted that he was better than the butterfly. The butterfly had once been wrapped up in the cocoon, but now he had ③ more freedom than the ant ever would.

The lesson learned here is that apparances can be deceptive.

page 1

Finding the Moral of the Story— "The Ant and the Chrysalis"

Directions: Read the text. Then, closely reread and annotate the text using colored pencils. Focus on the skill of finding the moral of the story. Underline or circle the sentences that help you find the moral of the story.

Close-Reading Tip

The moral of the story is the lesson that is learned. It usually focuses on positive messages. Circling key words will help you find the moral of the story.

The Ant and the Chrysalis— A Retelling of Aesop's Fable
by Dillon Autry

One summer day, an ant was running along the ground quickly. He was searching everywhere for some food. Then, he saw a chrysalis, which is a cocoon. The ant could tell from the large shape that the cocoon was near the end of its time. The ant saw the cocoon move. It was the first time the ant realized the cocoon was even alive.

"Poor, miserable bug," said the ant rudely. "How sad your life is. I can run hither and yonder, here and there. You can go nowhere at all. You are imprisoned where you are, but I can go wherever I want."

The cocoon heard every mean thing the ant said, but he did not reply.

A few days later, the ant walked by the cocoon again. He saw that only a shell was left. Suddenly, the ant felt a shadow pass over him. He looked up and saw a large, beautiful butterfly.

"Look at me now, Ant," said the butterfly. "Am I sad and miserable now? You can crawl on the ground or even up a tree, but without wings, you cannot fly from place to place." The ant knew that the butterfly was right. He should not have boasted that he was better than the butterfly. The butterfly had once been wrapped up in the cocoon, but now he had more freedom than the ant ever would.

page 1

Name _____ Date _____

Finding the Moral of the Story—
"The Ant and the Chrysalis" *(cont.)*

Directions: Read "The Ant and the Chrysalis—A Retelling of Aesop's Fable" on page 47, and respond to the questions.

> ### Remember!
> - Accurately answer the questions by stating your claim.
> - Provide evidence (direct quotation or paraphrasing) from the reading passage to support your answers.
> - Include at least one in-text citation (author, paragraph number).
> - Write a final thought to connect or further explain your answers.

1. What is the moral of the story? How do you know? Support your answer using evidence from the text.

   _____

   _____

   _____

2. How does the chrysalis get the final say with the ant?

   _____

   _____

   _____

3. What evidence from the text helps you understand what the author means when he says, "he had more freedom than the ant ever would"?

   _____

   _____

   _____

Determining Figurative Language

Materials

- *Determining Figurative Language—Annotation Example* (page 50; page50.pdf) (optional)

- copies of *Determining Figurative Language—"My Shadow"* (pages 51–52; page51.pdf)

- colored pencils

Procedure

1. Distribute *Determining Figurative Language—"My Shadow"* (pages 51–52), and have students read the passage independently.

2. Have students reread and complete a close reading and annotation of the poem using colored pencils. Students should focus specifically on the close-reading skill of identifying figurative language. Have students use one colored pencil to underline examples of similes and another colored pencil to underline examples of metaphors.

   - *Determining Figurative Language—Annotation Example* (page 50) can be used as reference, to model annotating for students, or as an individual scaffold for students as necessary.

Close-Reading Skill—Determining Figurative Language

Metaphors and similes are two of the most commonly used types of figurative language. Tell students to look for connecting words that help identify figurative language. For similes, students should look for the words *as* and *like*. For metaphors, students should look for comparisons using the word *is*.

3. Assign the text-dependent questions on page 52. Explain to students that their responses should accurately answer the questions, provide evidence (direct quotations or paraphrasing) from the reading passage to support the answers, include in-text citations, and conclude with final thoughts that connect or further explain the answers.

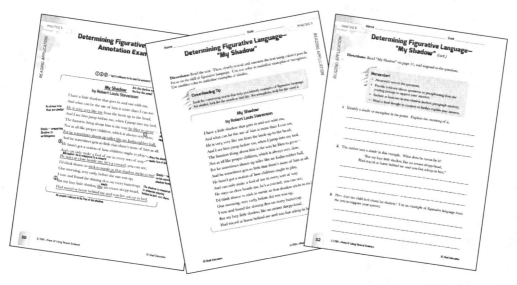

Determining Figurative Language—Annotation Example

①②③ = text evidence to be used in answers

My Shadow
Are the shadow and the boy the same?

by Robert Louis Stevenson

I have a little shadow that goes in and out with me,

And what can be the use of him is more than I can see.

He shows how they are similar
He is very, very like me from the heels up to the head;

And I see him jump before me, when I jump into my bed.

The funniest thing about him is the way he likes to grow—
Personification—he humanizes the shadow with his imagination.

Not at all like proper children, which is always very slow;
①

Simile— comparing Shadow to an India-rubber ball
For he sometimes shoots up taller like an India-rubber ball,

And he sometimes gets so little that there's none of him at all.

③He hasn't got a notion of how children ought to play,
Does the shadow make fun of him?

And can only make a fool of me in every sort of way.

Metaphor- he is compared to a coward.
He stays so close beside me, he's a coward, you can see;

I'd think shame to stick to nursie as that shadow sticks to me!
Simile— he doesn't hang on his nanny like the shadow hangs on him

One morning, very early, before the sun was up,

I rose and found the shining dew on every buttercup;
The shadow is compared to someone staying behind in bed- not there.

simile
②But my lazy little shadow, like an errant sleepy-head,

Had stayed at home behind me and was fast asleep in bed.

He sounds relieved to be free of his shadow.

Determining Figurative Language— "My Shadow"

Directions: Read the text. Then, closely reread and annotate the text using colored pencils. Focus on the skill of figurative language. Use one color to underline examples of metaphors. Use another color to underline examples of similes.

Close-Reading Tip

Look for connecting words that help you identify examples of figurative language. For similes, look for the words *as* and *like*. For metaphors, look for the word *is*.

My Shadow
by Robert Louis Stevenson

I have a little shadow that goes in and out with me,

And what can be the use of him is more than I can see.

He is very, very like me from the heels up to the head;

And I see him jump before me, when I jump into my bed.

The funniest thing about him is the way he likes to grow—

Not at all like proper children, which is always very slow;

For he sometimes shoots up taller like an India-rubber ball,

And he sometimes gets so little that there's none of him at all.

He hasn't got a notion of how children ought to play,

And can only make a fool of me in every sort of way.

He stays so close beside me, he's a coward, you can see;

I'd think shame to stick to nursie as that shadow sticks to me!

One morning, very early, before the sun was up,

I rose and found the shining dew on every buttercup;

But my lazy little shadow, like an errant sleepy-head,

Had stayed at home behind me and was fast asleep in bed.

Name _____ Date _____

Determining Figurative Language—
"My Shadow" *(cont.)*

Directions: Read "My Shadow" on page 51, and respond to the questions.

Remember!
- Accurately answer the questions by stating your claim.
- Provide evidence (direct quotation or paraphrasing) from the reading passage to support your answers.
- Include at least one in-text citation (author, paragraph number).
- Write a final thought to connect or further explain your answers.

1. Identify a simile or metaphor in the poem. Explain the meaning of it.

   _____

   _____

   _____

2. The author uses a simile in this example. What does he mean by it?

   "But my lazy little shadow, like an errant sleepy-head,
   Had stayed at home behind me and was fast asleep in bed."

   _____

   _____

   _____

3. How does the child feel about his shadow? Use an example of figurative language from the text to support your answer.

   _____

   _____

   _____

Analyzing Character

Materials

- copies of *Analyzing Character—Annotation Example* (page 54; page54.pdf) (optional)
- copies of *Analyzing Character—"Checkmate"* (pages 55–56; page55.pdf)
- colored pencils

Procedure

1. Distribute *Analyzing Character—"Checkmate"* (pages 55–56), and have students read the passage independently.

2. Have students reread and complete a close reading and annotation of the text using colored pencils. Students should focus specifically on the close-reading skill of analyzing characters. Have students use colored pencils to circle character traits as they read.

   - *Analyzing Character—Annotation Example* (page 54) can be used as reference, to model annotating for students, or as an individual scaffold for students as necessary.

Close-Reading Skill—Analyzing Characters

Begin by explaining to students that when analyzing a character, there are many traits to consider other than physical descriptions. Explain to students that traits can also include a character's feelings, beliefs, living environment, culture, or background.

3. Assign the text-dependent questions on page 56. Explain to students that their responses should accurately answer the question, provide evidence (direct quotations or paraphrasing) from the reading passage to support the answers, include in-text citations, and conclude with final thoughts that connect or further explain the answers.

4. Remind students that a citation is needed directly following a quotation. In this case, the abbreviation *par.* is used to reference a specific paragraph.

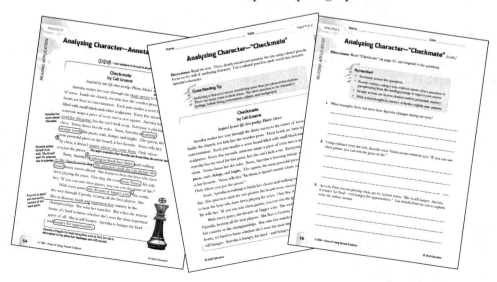

READING APPLICATION

Analyzing Character—Annotation Example

①②③ = text evidence to be used in answers

Checkmate
by Cali Greene

Inspired by real-life chess prodigy Phiona Mutesi

I picture a small town without paved streets, so maybe a place where people don't have a lot of money.

Ayeesha makes her way through the dusty streets to the center of town. Inside the church, ten kids line the wooden pews. Their heads are bent in concentration. Each pair studies a worn board filled with small black-and-white sculptures. Every few seconds, someone snaps a piece of ivory into a new square. Ayeesha has no word for this game, but she can't look away. Everyone is playing chess. Ventu shows her the rules. Soon, Ayeesha is learning strange words like *pawns*, *rooks*, *bishops*, and *knights*. The queen, the most powerful piece on the board, is her favorite. Ventu tells her, ③ "In chess, it doesn't matter where you come from. Only where you put the pieces."

Ayeesha has never played this game.

This might symbolize that Ayeesha can do anything she sets her mind to.

② Soon, Ayeesha is rushing to finish her chores and walking to the church every day. She practices until she can picture the board many moves ahead. She learns to beat the boys who have been playing for years. One day, she even beats Ventu. He tells her, "If you can win chess games, you can win the game of life."

Ayeesha pushes herself to do well. She doesn't wait for someone else to push her.

With every game, she dreams of bigger wins. ① She works her way through Uganda, beating all the best players. She flies to faraway lands and represents her country in the championships. She wins her matches. But when she returns home, it's hard to know whether she's won the most important game of all. She is still hungry. Ayeesha is hungry for food— and hungry for opportunities.

Ayeesha is smart and successful because of her hard work.

Ayeesha struggles for basic necessities such as food, but she is determined to rise above her challenges and still succeed.

Analyzing Character—"Checkmate"

Directions: Read the text. Then, closely reread and annotate the text using colored pencils. Focus on the skill of analyzing character. Use a colored pencil to circle words that describe Ayeesha's character.

Close-Reading Tip

Analyzing a character means considering more than just physical descriptions. There are many traits to think about. Pay close attention to the character's feelings, beliefs, living environment, culture, and background.

Checkmate
by Cali Greene
Inspired by real-life chess prodigy Phiona Mutesi

Ayeesha makes her way through the dusty streets to the center of town. Inside the church, ten kids line the wooden pews. Their heads are bent in concentration. Each pair studies a worn board filled with small black-and-white sculptures. Every few seconds, someone snaps a piece of ivory into a new square. Ayeesha has no word for this game, but she can't look away. Everyone is playing chess. Ventu shows her the rules. Soon, Ayeesha is learning strange words like *pawns*, *rooks*, *bishops*, and *knights*. The queen, the most powerful piece on the board, is her favorite. Ventu tells her, "In chess, it doesn't matter where you come from. Only where you put the pieces."

Soon, Ayeesha is rushing to finish her chores and walking to the church every day. She practices until she can picture the board many moves ahead. She learns to beat the boys who have been playing for years. One day, she even beats Ventu. He tells her, "If you can win chess games, you can win the game of life."

With every game, she dreams of bigger wins. She works her way through Uganda, beating all the best players. She flies to faraway lands and represents her country in the championships. She wins her matches. But when she returns home, it's hard to know whether she's won the most important game of all. She is still hungry. Ayeesha is hungry for food—and hungry for opportunities.

Analyzing Character—"Checkmate" (cont.)

Directions: Read "Checkmate" on page 55, and respond to the questions.

> ### Remember!
> - Accurately answer the questions by stating your claim.
> - Provide evidence using a text evidence starter (direct quotation or paraphrasing) from the reading passage to support your answer.
> - Include at least one in-text citation (author, paragraph number).
> - Write a final thought to connect or further explain your answers.

1. What examples from text show how Ayeesha changes during the story?

   _____

   _____

   _____

2. Using evidence from the text, describe what Ventu means when he says, "If you can win chess games, you can win the game of life."

   _____

   _____

   _____

3. Ayeesha finds success playing chess, yet the author states, "She is still hungry. Ayeesha is hungry for food—and hungry for opportunities." Use details from the text to explain what the author means.

   _____

   _____

   _____

Determining Main Idea

Materials

- *Determining Main Idea—Annotation Example* (page 58; page58.pdf) (optional)
- copies of *Determining Main Idea—"Go-Kart Racing"* (pages 59–60; page59.pdf)
- colored pencils
- a pencil

Procedure

1. Distribute *Determining Main Idea—"Go-Kart Racing"* (pages 59–60), and have students read the passage independently.

2. Have students reread and complete a close reading and annotation of the text using colored pencils. Students should focus specifically on the close-reading skill of determining the main idea. Have students use colored pencils to underline details about the main idea in each paragraph.

3. Tell students to use the underlined details to identify the main idea of each paragraph. Have them write the main idea in the margins next to the paragraphs.

   - *Determining Main Idea—Annotation Example* (page 58) can be used as reference, to model annotating for students, or as an individual scaffold for students as necessary.

Close-Reading Skill—Determining Main Idea

Explain to students that the main idea is the overall idea of a text. It is sometimes easily found, and other times it is more difficult. Tell students that identifying details will help determine the main idea of a text.

4. Assign the text-dependent questions on page 60. Explain to students that their responses should accurately answer the question, provide evidence (direct quotations or paraphrasing) from the reading passage to support the answers, include in-text citations, and conclude with final thoughts that connect or further describe the answers.

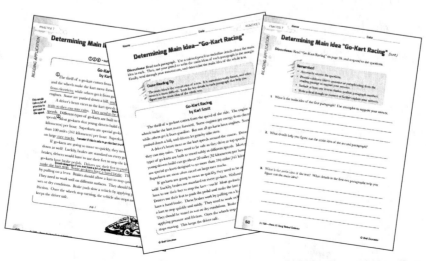

Determining Main Idea—Annotation Example

①②③ = text evidence to be used in answers

Go-Kart Racing
by Karl Scott

Main Idea
This sentence tells us about what the whole paragraph is about.

①The thrill of a go-kart comes from the speed of the ride. The engine and the wheels make the kart move forward. Some engines get energy from electricity, while others get it from gasoline. ③But not all go-karts have engines. Some are pushed down a hill, and drivers let gravity take over.

This sounds both fun and scary!

A driver's heart races as the kart speeds around the course. Drivers train so they can stay calm. They need to be safe as they drive at top

Main Idea

speeds. Different types of go-karts are built to travel safely at different speeds. ②Most go-karts that young drivers build can go about 20 miles (32 kilometers) per hour. Superkarts are special go-karts designed to go more than 100 miles (161 kilometers) per hour. Superkarts are most often raced on large race tracks. *I wonder if this is safe to go this fast in a Go-Kart?*

This would take a lot of practice to get used to the speed.

How old do you have to be to drive a Go-Kart? Do you have to have a driver's license?

If go-karts are going to move so quickly, they need to be able to slow down as well! Luckily, brakes are standard on every go-kart. Without brakes, drivers would have to use their feet to stop the kart—ouch! ③Most go-karts have brake pedals. Drivers use their feet to push the pedal and make the kart stop. Some go-karts have a hand brake. These brakes work

Sounds dangerous if you dont have a lot of practice.

by pulling on a lever. Brakes should allow a kart to stop quickly and safely. They need to work well on different surfaces. They should be tested in wet or dry conditions. Brake pads slow a vehicle by applying pressure and friction. Once the wheels stop turning, the vehicle also stops moving. This keeps the driver safe.

page 1

Determining Main Idea—"Go-Kart Racing"

Directions: Read the text. Use a colored pencil to underline details about the main idea in each paragraph. Then, use your pencil to write the main idea of each paragraph in the margin. Finally, read through your annotations, and determine the main idea of the whole text.

Close-Reading Tip

The main idea is the overall idea of a text. It is sometimes easily found, and other times it is more difficult. Look for key details in each paragraph that help you figure out the main idea of the whole text.

Go-Kart Racing
by Karl Scott

The thrill of a go-kart comes from the speed of the ride. The engine and the wheels make the kart move forward. Some engines get energy from electricity, while others get it from gasoline. But not all go-karts have engines. Some are pushed down a hill, and drivers let gravity take over.

A driver's heart races as the kart speeds around the course. Drivers train so they can stay calm. They need to be safe as they drive at top speeds. Different types of go-karts are built to travel safely at different speeds. Most go-karts that young drivers build can go about 20 miles (32 kilometers) per hour. Superkarts are special go-karts designed to go more than 100 miles (161 kilometers) per hour. Superkarts are most often raced on large race tracks.

If go-karts are going to move so quickly, they need to be able to slow down as well! Luckily, brakes are standard on every go-kart. Without brakes, drivers would have to use their feet to stop the kart—ouch! Most go-karts have brake pedals. Drivers use their feet to push the pedal and make the kart stop. Some go-karts have a hand brake. These brakes work by pulling on a lever. Brakes should allow a kart to stop quickly and safely. They need to work well on different surfaces. They should be tested in wet or dry conditions. Brake pads slow a vehicle by applying pressure and friction. Once the wheels stop turning, the vehicle also stops moving. This keeps the driver safe.

page 1

READING APPLICATION

Determining Main Idea "Go-Kart Racing" *(cont.)*

Directions: Read "Go-Kart Racing" on page 59, and respond to the questions.

> ### Remember!
> - Accurately answer the questions by stating your claim.
> - Provide evidence (direct quotation or paraphrasing) from the reading passage to support your answers.
> - Include at least one in-text citation (author, paragraph number).
> - Write a final thought to connect or further explain your answers.

1. What is the main idea of the first paragraph? Use examples to support your answer.

   _____

   _____

   _____

2. What details help you figure out the main idea of the third paragraph?

   _____

   _____

   _____

3. What is the main idea of the whole text? What details in the first two paragraphs help you figure this out?

   _____

   _____

   _____

   _____

Identifying Author's Purpose

✏️ Materials

- *Identifying Author's Purpose—Annotation Example* (page 62; page62.pdf) (optional)
- copies of *Identifying Author's Purpose—"A Beginner's Guide to Soccer"* (pages 63–64; page63.pdf)
- colored pencils

Procedure

1. Distribute *Identifying Author's Purpose—"A Beginner's Guide to Soccer"* (pages 63–64), and have students read the passage independently.

2. Have students reread and complete a close reading and annotation of the text. Students can focus specifically on the close-reading skill of identifying author's purpose. Have students use colored pencils to circle or underline key details that help them identify the author's purpose.

   - *Identifying Author's Purpose—Annotation Example* (page 62) can be used as reference, to model annotating for students, or as an individual scaffold for students as necessary.

Close-Reading Skill—Identifying Author's Purpose

Explain to students that there are three main types of author's purpose: persuasive, informative, and explanatory. Tell students to look for key words that could be clues to the author's purpose. Italicized words would most likely be persuasive. Factual and organizational words are used to inform or explain, and descriptive words help with expression.

3. Assign the text-dependent questions on page 64. Explain to students that their responses should accurately answer the questions, provide evidence (direct quotations or paraphrasing) from the reading passage to support the answers, include in-text citations, and conclude with final thoughts that connect or further explain the answers.

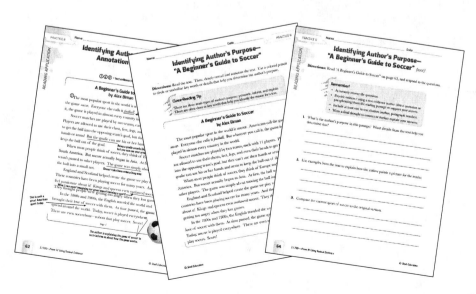

Identifying Author's Purpose— Annotation Example

①②③ = text evidence to be used in answers

A Beginner's Guide to Soccer
by Alex Biman

①The most popular sport in the world is soccer. Americans call the game *soccer*. Everyone else calls it *football*. But whatever you call it, the game is played in almost every country in the world.

Why do Americans have a differnt word for it? That's confusing!

Soccer matches are played by two teams, each with 11 players. Players are allowed to use their chest, feet, legs, and even their heads to get the ball into the opposing team's goal, but they can't use their hands or arms! But the goalie can use his or her hands and arms to keep the ball out of the goal.

Being a goalie sounds like the hardest job, but you can use your arms and hands.

When most people think of soccer, they think of Europe and South America. But soccer actually began in Asia. At first, the ball wasn't passed to other players. The game was simply about ③ moving the ball into a small net.

Soccer rules have come a long way.

England and Scotland helped create the game we play today. These countries have been playing soccer for many years. And they feel passionate about it! Kings and queens even outlawed soccer.②

Wow, I can never imagining our government banning a sport!

They thought people were getting too angry when they lost games.

In the 1800s and 1900s, the English traveled the world and brought their love of soccer with them. As time passed, the game spread around the world. Today, soccer is played everywhere. There are even soccerbots—robots that play soccer. Score!

This is such a great American sport today.

page 1

The author is explaining the game of soccer to us to inform us about how the game works.

Identifying Author's Purpose—
"A Beginner's Guide to Soccer"

Directions: Read the text. Then, closely reread and annotate the text. Use a colored pencil to circle or underline key words or details that help you determine the author's purpose.

Close-Reading Tip

There are three main types of author's purpose: persuade, inform, and explain. There are often clues or key words that help you identify the reason for a text.

A Beginner's Guide to Soccer
by Alex Biman

The most popular sport in the world is soccer. Americans call the game *soccer*. Everyone else calls it *football*. But whatever you call it, the game is played in almost every country in the world.

Soccer matches are played by two teams, each with 11 players. Players are allowed to use their chest, feet, legs, and even their heads to get the ball into the opposing team's goal, but they can't use their hands or arms! But the goalie can use his or her hands and arms to keep the ball out of the goal.

When most people think of soccer, they think of Europe and South America. But soccer actually began in Asia. At first, the ball wasn't passed to other players. The game was simply about moving the ball into a small net.

England and Scotland helped create the game we play today. These countries have been playing soccer for many years. And they feel passionate about it! Kings and queens even outlawed soccer. They thought people were getting too angry when they lost games.

In the 1800s and 1900s, the English traveled the world and brought their love of soccer with them. As time passed, the game spread around the world. Today, soccer is played everywhere. There are even soccerbots—robots that play soccer. Score!

page 1

Identifying Author's Purpose—
"A Beginner's Guide to Soccer" *(cont.)*

Directions: Read "A Beginner's Guide to Soccer" on page 63, and respond to the questions.

Remember!
- Accurately answer the questions.
- Provide evidence using a text evidence starter (direct quotation or paraphrasing) from the reading passage to support your answer.
- Include at least one in-text citation (author, paragraph number).
- Write a final thought to connect or further explain your answers.

1. What is the author's purpose in this passage? What details from the text help you determine this?

   _____

   _____

   _____

2. Use examples from the text to explain how the author paints a picture for the reader.

   _____

   _____

   _____

3. Compare the current sport of soccer to the original version.

   _____

   _____

   _____

Studying Text Structure

✎ Materials

- *Studying Text Structure—Annotation Example* (page 66; page66.pdf) (optional)
- copies of *Studying Text Structure—"How to Blow Bigger Bubbles"* (pages 67–68; page67.pdf)
- colored pencils

Procedure

1. Distribute *Studying Text Structure—"How to Blow Bigger Bubbles"* (pages 67–68), and have students read the passage independently.

2. Have students skim the passage first, looking for signal words that will help identify how the text is organized. Then, have students use colored pencils to put boxes around the key words that help identify structure.

   - *Studying Text Structure—Annotation Example* (page 66) can be used as reference, to model annotating for students, or as an individual scaffold for students as necessary.

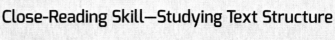

Close-Reading Skill—Studying Text Structure

Explain to students that text structure is how the information is organized. Text structure includes the following frameworks: compare and contrast, description, problem and solution, chronological, sequence, cause and effect, and directions.

3. Assign the text-dependent questions on page 68. Explain to students that their responses should accurately answer the questions, provide evidence (direct quotations or paraphrasing) from the reading passage to support the answers, include in-text citations, and conclude with final thoughts that connect or further explain the answers.

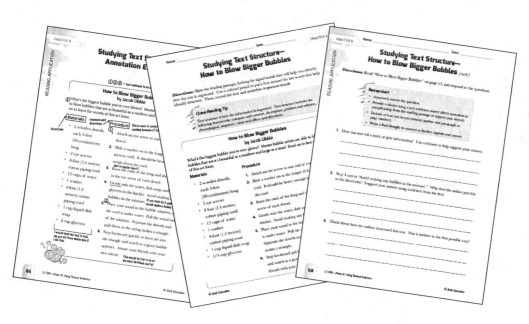

Studying Text Structure—
Annotation Example

①②③ = text evidence to be used in answers

How to Blow Bigger Bubbles
by Jacob Ubble

③ What's the biggest bubble you've ever blown? Master bubble artists are able to blow bubbles that are as beautiful as a rainbow and large as a man! Read on to learn the secrets of this art form.

Materials	*sequence and directions*

directions

- 2 wooden dowels, each 3-feet (30-centimeters) long
- 2 eye screws
- 8-foot (2.4 meters) cotton piping cord
- 12 cups of water
- 1 washer
- 4-foot (1.2 meters) cotton piping cord
- 1 cup liquid dish soap
- ¼ cup glycerin

I would need my dad to help me get all these materials if I did this.

Procedure	*This is easy to understand before I start reading because of how it's organized.*

① 1. Attach an eye screw to one end of each dowel.

2. Slide a washer on to the longer (8-foot, 2.4 meters) cord. It should be heavy enough to weigh down the cord.

I might need help to do some of these steps.

Just a regular knot?

3. Knot the ends of the long and short cords in the eye screw of each dowel.

4. Gently mix the water, dish soap, and glycerin in the bucket. Avoid making any bubbles in the mixture.

If you don't do it gently, I think it would make a bubble mess.

② 5. Place your wand in the bubble solution, so the cord is under water. Pull the wand out of the solution. Separate the dowels and pull down so the string makes a triangle.

6. Step backward quickly to force air into the triangle and watch as a giant bubble appears. Amaze your friends with your new talent!

This would be fun to do at my next birthday party!

Studying Text Structure— "How to Blow Bigger Bubbles"

Directions: Skim the reading passage, looking for signal words that will help you identify how the text is organized. Use a colored pencil to put a box around the key words that help identify structure. Then, reread the text and underline important details.

Close-Reading Tip

Text structure is how the information is organized. Text structure includes the following frameworks: compare and contrast, description, problem and solution, chronological, sequence, cause and effect, and directions.

How to Blow Bigger Bubbles
by Jacob Ubble

What's the biggest bubble you've ever blown? Master bubble artists are able to blow bubbles that are as beautiful as a rainbow and large as a man! Read on to learn the secrets of this art form.

Materials

- 2 wooden dowels, each 3-feet (30-centimeters) long
- 2 eye screws
- 8-foot (2.4 meters) cotton piping cord
- 12 cups of water
- 1 washer
- 4-foot (1.2 meters) cotton piping cord
- 1 cup liquid dish soap
- $\frac{1}{4}$ cup glycerin

Procedure

1. Attach an eye screw to one end of each dowel.
2. Slide a washer on to the longer (8-foot, 2.4 meters) cord. It should be heavy enough to weigh down the cord.
3. Knot the ends of the long and short cords in the eye screw of each dowel.
4. Gently mix the water, dish soap, and glycerin in the bucket. Avoid making any bubbles in the mixture.
5. Place your wand in the bubble solution, so the cord is under water. Pull the wand out of the solution. Separate the dowels and pull down so the string makes a triangle.
6. Step backward quickly to force air into the triangle and watch as a giant bubble appears. Amaze your friends with your new talent!

Name _____ Date _____

Studying Text Structure—
"How to Blow Bigger Bubbles" (cont.)

Directions: Read "How to Blow Bigger Bubbles" on page 67, and respond to the questions.

> ### Remember!
> • Accurately answer the question by stating your claim.
> • Provide evidence using a text evidence starter (direct quotation or paraphrasing) from the reading passage to support your answer.
> • Include at least one in-text citation (author and paragraph or page number).
> • Write a final thought to connect or further explain your answer.

1. Does this text tell a story or give information? Use evidence to help support your answer.

   _____

   _____

   _____

2. Step 4 says to "Avoid making any bubbles in the mixture." Why does the author put this in the directions? Support your answer using evidence from the text.

   _____

   _____

   _____

3. Think about how the author structured this text. Was it written in the best possible way?

   _____

   _____

   _____

Comparing and Contrasting

✏ Materials

- *Comparing and Contrasting—Annotation Example* (page 70; page70.pdf) (optional)

- copies of *Comparing and Contrasting—Excerpt from "Circuits"* (pages 71–72; page71.pdf)

- colored pencils

Procedure

1. Distribute copies of *Comparing and Contrasting—Excerpt from "Circuits"* (pages 71–72). Explain to students that as they read, they will be identifying similarities and differences.

2. Have students read the passage independently. Have each student use one colored pencil to underline details that are similar and use another colored pencil to underline differences.

   - *Comparing and Contrasting—Annotation Example* (page 70) can be used as reference, to model annotating for students, or as an individual scaffold for students as necessary.

Close-Reading Skill—Comparing and Contrasting

Explain to students that comparing and contrasting is finding the similarities and differences between two or more texts. Using different colored pens or pencils will help keep their thoughts organized.

3. Assign the text-dependent questions on page 72. Explain to students that their responses should accurately answer the question, provide evidence (direct quotations or paraphrasing) from the reading passage to support the answers, include in-text citations, and conclude with final thoughts that connect or further explain the answers.

4. Remind students that a citation is needed directly following a quotation. In this case, the abbreviation *par.* is used to reference a specific paragraph.

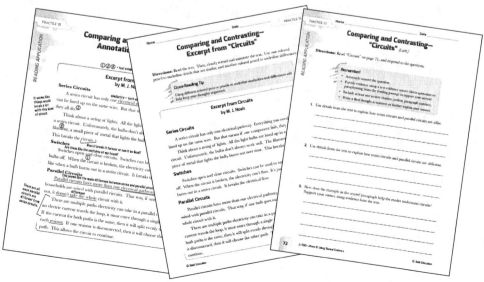

Comparing and Contrasting— Annotation Example

①②③ = text evidence to be used in answers

Excerpt from "Circuits"
by M. J. Noah

Series Circuits

similarity— both electrical pathways

A series circuit has only one electrical pathway. Everything you need can be lined up on the same wire. But that means if one component fails, they all do.②

It seems like things would break a lot with this kind of circuit.

Think about a string of lights. All the light bulbs are lined up in a series circuit. Unfortunately, the bulbs don't always work well. The filament③, a small piece of metal that lights the bulb, burns out over time. This breaks the circuit.

Does it break it forever or can it be fixed?

Switches

Are these like the switches at my house?

Switches open and close circuits.① Switches can be used to turn light bulbs off. When the circuit is broken, the electricity can't flow. It's just like when a bulb burns out in a series circuit. It breaks the electrical flow.

Parallel Circuits

This seems like the main difference between series and parallel circuits.

Parallel circuits have more than one electrical pathway. Most households are wired with parallel circuits. That way, if one bulb goes out, it *difference* doesn't take the whole circuit with it.

These are all ways parallel circuits are different from series circuits.

There are multiple paths electricity can take in a parallel circuit. As an electric current travels the loop, it must enter through a single resistor. If the current for both paths is the same, then it will split evenly through each resistor. If one resistor is disconnected, then it will choose the other path. This allows the circuit to continue.

Comparing and Contrasting— Excerpt from "Circuits"

Directions: Read the text. Then, closely reread and annotate the text. Use one colored pencil to underline details that are similar, and another colored pencil to underline differences.

Close-Reading Tip

Using different colored pens or pencils to underline similarities and differences will help keep your thoughts organized.

Excerpt from "Circuits"
by M. J. Noah

Series Circuits

A series circuit has only one electrical pathway. Everything you need can be lined up on the same wire. But that means if one component fails, they all do.

Think about a string of lights. All the light bulbs are lined up in a series circuit. Unfortunately, the bulbs don't always work well. The filament, a small piece of metal that lights the bulb, burns out over time. This breaks the circuit.

Switches

Switches open and close circuits. Switches can be used to turn light bulbs off. When the circuit is broken, the electricity can't flow. It's just like when a bulb burns out in a series circuit. It breaks the electrical flow.

Parallel Circuits

Parallel circuits have more than one electrical pathway. Most households are wired with parallel circuits. That way, if one bulb goes out, it doesn't take the whole circuit with it.

There are multiple paths electricity can take in a parallel circuit. As an electric current travels the loop, it must enter through a single resistor. If the current for both paths is the same, then it will split evenly through each resistor. If one resistor is disconnected, then it will choose the other path. This allows the circuit to continue.

Comparing and Contrasting—
Excerpt from "Circuits" (cont.)

Directions: Read Excerpt from "Circuits" on page 71, and respond to the questions.

> **Remember!**
> • Accurately answer the question.
> • Provide evidence using a text evidence starter (direct quotation or paraphrasing) from the reading passage to support your answer.
> • Include at least one in-text citation (author, paragraph number).
> • Write a final thought to connect or further explain your answer.

1. Use details from the text to explain how series circuits and parallel circuits are alike.

   _____

   _____

   _____

2. Use details from the text to explain how series circuits and parallel circuits are different.

   _____

   _____

   _____

3. How does the example in the second paragraph help the reader understand circuits? Support your answer using evidence from the text.

   _____

   _____

   _____

   _____

Writing Lessons and Application

Textual Evidence in Writing

Lesson 6: Gathering Sources 75

Lesson 7: Supporting a Claim 78

Lesson 8: Organizing Evidence 81

Lesson 9: Writing an Analysis 84

Lesson 10: Listing Sources 87

Writing Application Prompts

Prompt 1: Description Text Structure 90

Prompt 2: Sequence Text Structure 93

Prompt 3: Compare-and-Contrast Text Structure 96

Prompt 4: Compare-and-Contrast Text Structure 99

Prompt 5: Cause-and-Effect Text Structure 102

Prompt 6: Description Text Structure 105

Prompt 7: Problem-and-Solution Text Structure 108

Prompt 8: Chronological Text Structure 111

Prompt 9: Classification Text Structure 114

Prompt 10: Sequence Text Structure 117

Gathering Sources

Objective

Students will search for and gather credible and reliable sources for research.

Materials

- copies of *Gathering Sources Practice 1* (page 76; page76.pdf)
- copies of *Gathering Sources Practice 2* (page 77; page77.pdf)

Essential Question

How do I gather credible and reliable sources for research?

Guided Practice

1. Distribute copies of *Gathering Sources Practice 1* (page 76). Begin by defining what a source is (a text or an image you can use to learn about a topic) and explaining the difference between print and digital sources. Have students write these definitions on their activity sheets.

2. Students should understand that they can look on the Internet for sources about a topic, but they should be careful. Some things will not be what they are looking for, and some sites will not be credible (true; able to be believed) or reliable (able to be trusted; typically supported by experts). Students should write the definitions of *credible* and *reliable* on their activity sheets.

3. Explain to students that when they need to do research, they should type in keywords to find what they need. They should only type in the main keywords about their topics. If they type too many words, the search returns might be too varied.

4. Work through number 5 with students as an example. Get suggested search terms from students, and type them into a search engine. Have students look at the list of options that come up for the search results. Go through each option with students, and discuss which websites would be reliable and credible, which would not, and why.

5. Explain to students that they should never click on websites that require them to be a certain age, have inappropriate material, or ask them to give away personal information.

6. Allow time for students to complete the rest of the practice sheet in pairs or small groups.

Independent Practice

- Have students complete *Gathering Sources Practice 2* (page 77) in class, as homework, or as an assessment to ensure they can complete the skill independently.

Additional Support

Allow extra time for students to practice visiting reliable and unreliable websites to compare and contrast the differences.

GUIDED PRACTICE

Gathering Sources Practice 1

Directions: Define the vocabulary words related to the word *source*.

1. print source: _____

2. digital source: _____

3. reliable source: _____

4. credible source: _____

Directions: Write in which keywords you would use to search for each topic described.

5. You want to research the best places to go on vacation for families with kids.

    _____

6. You want to know the names of how to make homemade macaroni and cheese.

    _____

7. You want to find out about what you need to know to adopt a puppy.

    _____

Directions: State which sources appear to be reliable and credible by writing "Yes" or "No" next to each example.

_____ 8. **www.humanesocietyadoption.com**
                      Whether you want a senior dog or a playful puppy, we can help you find the perfect dog to match your needs.

_____ 9. **www.blogging4fun.com/mynewpup**
                      I love my puppppppy! I took him to the park and we played for an hour, but then he ran away from me and …

_____ 10. **www.wikipedia.com/adoptingapuppy**
                       When buying a new puppy, you should always make sure the puppy has gotten shots to keep it …

Gathering Sources Practice 2

Directions: Write in the keywords you would use to search for the topic described.

1. You want to research where World War II was fought.

   _____

2. You want to find out what you need to make friendship bracelets.

   _____

3. You want to find out about the strangest bugs in the United States.

   _____

4. You want to know the names of the tallest buildings in the world.

   _____

Directions: State which sources appear to be reliable and credible about the tallest buildings in the world by writing "Yes" or "No" next to each example.

_____ 5. **www.makingmodelbuildings123.com**

You can build any building you want in your own home by the click of a button! Ships quickly!

_____ 6. **www.newsnow.com**

The buildings get bigger and bigger each year, and we have the top ten buildings from around the world showcased.

_____ 7. **www.architecture4today.com**

Travel through the most beautiful buildings of today.

Tip: Be sure your sources are reliable and credible. If you are unsure, check at least two other sources to see if the information matches. If it doesn't, that source is probably not reliable and/or credible.

Supporting a Claim

🔍 Objective

Students will understand how to support a claim by drawing relevant evidence and using logical reasoning.

✏️ Materials

- copies of *Supporting a Claim Practice 1* (page 79; page79.pdf)
- copies of *Supporting a Claim Practice 2* (page 80; page80.pdf)

💡 Essential Question

How do I support a claim using logical reasoning and relevant evidence?

Guided Practice

1. Begin by explaining that when you make a claim about a topic, you should support it with arguments to show that what you are saying holds value. This can be done by supporting the claim with logical reasoning and relevant evidence.

    - Logical reasoning is a statement that makes a claim make sense.

    - Relevant evidence is facts that come from sources.

2. Have students imagine they are going to be writing about whether video games should be considered a sport.

3. Distribute *Supporting a Claim Practice 1* (page 79). Have students read each example and follow the directions. As a class, talk through each example to help students better understand how to support claims.

4. Explain to students that although a sentence sometimes does not have logical reasoning or relevant evidence, it is still useful to include. An example of this would be a topic statement.

5. Explain to students that they should not only rely on logical reasoning or relevant evidence, but they should also use their own background knowledge on the subject to support their claims.

Independent Practice

- Have students complete *Supporting a Claim Practice 2* (page 80) in class, as homework, or as an assessment to ensure they can complete the skill independently.

Additional Support

Give students a list of reliable online sources to use or encourage them to go to a library and find reliable printed sources.

Supporting a Claim Practice 1

Directions: Read the text. Then, for each statement, fill in the line using the correct letters:

LR—Logical Reasoning   RE—Relevant Evidence   N—Neither

Should Video Games Be Considered a Sport?

Gaming is definitely a sport in today's world. Just like a physical sport, it takes learning skills and using strategy. It can be played individually or on a team. Video games are also fun. There are even worldwide tournaments. Games require players to be mentally strong and focused. They also need to have quick reaction times. Just like in sports, players in tournaments have many fans that cheer them on. Sometimes, gaming draws more viewers than traditional sports. One tournament had more than 12 million viewers. Some sports may only have a couple dozen people show up to watch.

_____ **1.** Gaming is definitely a sport in today's world.

_____ **2.** Just like a sport, it takes learning skills and using strategy.

_____ **3.** It can be played individually or on a team.

_____ **4.** Video games are also fun.

_____ **5.** There are even worldwide tournaments.

_____ **6.** Games require players to be mentally strong and focused.

_____ **7.** They also need to have quick reaction times.

_____ **8.** Just like sports, players in tournaments have many fans that cheer them on, sometimes drawing more viewers than other sports.

_____ **9.** Sometimes, gaming draws more views than traditional sports.

_____ **10.** One tournament had more than 12 million viewers.

_____ **11.** Some sports may have only a couple dozen people show up to watch.

INDEPENDENT PRACTICE

Supporting a Claim Practice 2

Directions: Read the text. Then, for each statement, fill in the line using the correct letters:

LR—Logical Reasoning   **RE—Relevant Evidence**   **N—Neither**

Should Graffiti be Considered Art?

Art is thought to be the human expression of imagination. If so, then graffiti should be thought of as an art form. Graffiti is messy for workers to clean up. Some workers don't get paid very well to clean it off walls. For a long time, graffiti was thought to be ugly. Graffiti now involves more than just words. Graffiti can be a symbol of the people in the city. Some people are trained in certain types of graffiti. People can even take classes at local community colleges.

_____ 1. Art is thought to be the human expression of imagination.

_____ 2. If so, then graffiti should be thought of as an art form.

_____ 3. Graffiti is messy for workers to clean up.

_____ 4. Some workers don't get paid very well to clean it off walls.

_____ 5. For a long time, graffiti was thought to be ugly.

_____ 6. Graffiti now involves more than just words.

_____ 7. Graffiti can be a symbol of the people in the city.

_____ 8. Some people are trained in certain types of graffiti.

_____ 9. People can even take classes at local community colleges.

Tip: Remember that logical reasoning is a statement that makes a claim make sense. Relevant evidence is a fact from an outside source that supports a claim.

Organizing Evidence

🔍 Objective

Students will organize evidence into categories before beginning writing.

✏️ Materials

- copies of *Organizing Evidence Practice 1* (page 82; page82.pdf)
- copies of *Organizing Evidence Practice 2* (page 83; page83.pdf)

💡 Essential Question

How do I organize my research into categories for prewriting?

Guided Practice

1. Begin by explaining to students that when you are writing about a topic and have claims to support that topic, you should organize the facts and opinions into categories so your writing will be organized.

2. Tell students they will read a list of notes taken from articles about pet monkeys that are either logical reasoning or relevant evidence. They have to categorize these notes into three main categories about the topic, which is "Monkeys Make Terrible Pets!"

3. Distribute copies of *Organizing Evidence Practice 1* (page 82). Have students read through the statements and come up with logical categories.

4. Explain to students that they should not simply list facts as support in the order that they think of them or find them, but that claims should always be organized into bigger categories that have evidence to back them up.

Independent Practice

- Have students complete *Organizing Evidence Practice 2* (page 83) in class, as homework, or as an assessment to ensure they can complete the skill independently.

Additional Support

Have students highlight information and write a letter or number next to the text to represent each category.

Organizing Evidence Practice 1

Directions: Read each note about pet monkeys. Then, come up with ways the notes could be categorized into three main topics. Rewrite each note in the correct column of the chart.

Monkeys Make Terrible Pets!
- Monkeys will require you to stay home more to take care of them.
- Monkeys will bite humans.
- You must buy a license to have a monkey.
- Monkeys can damage property when left alone.
- Monkeys need a lot of attention.
- You must buy food and other materials for monkeys.
- Monkeys will fly into rages.
- Monkeys require veterinarian checks that can be expensive.
- Monkeys can be jealous of other animals or people.

Topic A: _____	Topic B: _____	Topic C: _____

Name _____ Date _____

Organizing Evidence Practice 2

Directions: Read each note about Johnny Appleseed. Then, come up with ways the notes could be categorized into three main topics. Rewrite each note in the correct column of the chart.

The Life of Johnny Appleseed
- He died in 1845.
- He developed a successful business.
- He headed out West with the settlers.
- He spent much of his life planting apple seeds when he traveled.
- He wanted to help the settlers arriving at the new land.
- He was born in 1774.
- He lived and slept outdoors.
- He didn't spend a lot of money.
- He is a famous American folk hero.

Topic A: _____ **Topic B:** _____ **Topic C:** _____

Tip: Remember that the facts should be organized into similar topics before you begin writing so that the writing will make sense to the reader.

Writing an Analysis

🔍 Objective

Students will write organized and supported analyses using textual evidence.

✏️ Materials

- copies of *Writing an Analysis Practice* (pages 85–86; page85.pdf)

💡 Essential Question

How do I put together an organized and supported analysis after reading a text?

Guided Practice

1. Explain to students they will read a short text about the disadvantages of homework, and then they will write short essays about why kids shouldn't have homework. Remind students that they may not agree with what they are writing, but they should stay on topic.

2. To organize their essays, students should have four paragraphs. The first should be two or three sentences stating the topic. The next two paragraphs should discuss two main reasons why students should not have homework. These paragraphs should have supporting details cited correctly. The final paragraph should conclude with a summary statement of two to three sentences. (It would be a good idea to draw this organization on the board so students can see how to organize their essays.)

3. Distribute *Writing an Analysis Practice* (pages 85–86). Have students annotate on the text on page 85 as well as take notes as needed on separate sheets of paper. These annotations and notes will be used later for text citations.

4. They should then take time to use their annotations, notes, and their own logical reasoning to organize their thinking before they write their essays. They need to come up with two clear reasons and supporting details and quotations that defend the view that students should not have homework.

5. Explain to students that they should not include everything from the article. Instead, they should use evidence that will most clearly support their two main reasons. Remind students they should use exact words and phrases from the text as part of their evidence. Students should have a minimum of two in-text citations.

Independent Practice

- Have students complete *Writing an Analysis Practice* (page 86) in class, as homework, or as an assessment to ensure they can complete the skill independently.

Additional Support

Encourage students to highlight the evidence in the article as they go, or have it highlighted for them, so they can see what would be good examples of evidence in the text.

Writing an Analysis Practice

Directions: Read the information in the chart. Annotate the text by underlining key words. Then, in the chart at the bottom of the page, write ideas from the list and your own ideas to prepare for your written response.

Pros and Cons to Homework
by Max Pencil

Pros	Cons
• Homework improves study skills. • Homework teaches time management. • Homework encourages parental involvement. • Homework teaches being independent. • Practice helps some students learn better.	• Homework takes up too much family time. • Homework creates frustration and stress. • Kids are busy with sports and other activities. • Kids might practice the wrong way if the teacher isn't there. • Some students might not have supplies or technology at home to do the homework. • No research shows that homework improves grades. • Homework can be boring. • Some parents don't know enough to help students on their homework.

Reason: _____	Reason: _____

Name _____ Date _____

Writing an Analysis Practice *(cont.)*

Directions: Use the chart from page 85 to write a four-paragraph essay about why students should not have homework.

_____

_____

_____

_____

_____

_____

_____

_____

_____

_____

_____

_____

_____

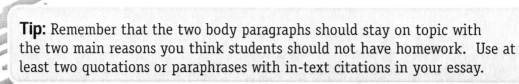

Tip: Remember that the two body paragraphs should stay on topic with the two main reasons you think students should not have homework. Use at least two quotations or paraphrases with in-text citations in your essay.

Listing Sources

🔍 Objective

Students will list sources from the in-text citations as a bibliography (also called works cited or references cited). **Note:** *Talk to your local curriculum director to find which preferred style would be most applicable for your students.*

✏️ Materials

- copies of *Listing Sources Practice 1* (page 88; page88.pdf)
- copies of *Listing Sources Practice 2* (page 89; page89.pdf)

💡 Essential Question

How do I make a list of sources that I have used for in-text citations?

Guided Practice

1. Explain to students that when they write essays, they must create a list of the sources they used to help write their papers. In MLA format, the list should be titled *Bibliography* and should include the sources in alphabetical order by the authors' last names. While listing sources in MLA style is more thorough, the list can be simplified as needed.

Bibliography

Book	Author Last Name, First Name. *Title.* Publisher.
Encyclopedia or other article	Author Last Name, First Name. "Title." *Name of Magazine* or Publisher.
Online source	Author or website creator (if found). "Title of Article." *Main Website Name.* URL.

2. Distribute *Listing Sources Practice 1* (page 88). Have students practice listing sources by completing the activity sheet.

3. Explain to students that they should not change the format listed. When there is a period, use a period; and when there is a comma, use a comma. Guide students in correct formatting as needed.

Independent Practice

- Have students complete *Listing Sources Practice 2* (page 89) in class, as homework, or as an assessment to ensure they can complete the skill independently.

Additional Support

Work with students to name aloud each component of the entry (i.e., author last name, author first name). This will help them keep the different parts straight.

GUIDED PRACTICE

Name _____ Date _____

Listing Sources Practice 1

Directions: Pretend you wrote an essay about interesting bugs and used these sources. Write the listing for each source. Then, number the entries to show the correct order for a bibliography.

Strange Bugs
By Buddy Creature

published by
Allen Publishing

_____

_____

_____

Big Bugs of the Northwest
By Julie Flyer

National Bug Magazine

_____

_____

_____

www.weirdbugsandinsects.com

Weird Bugs and Insects

Bugs Big and Small
By George Beetle

_____

_____

_____

Listing Sources Practice 2

Directions: Pretend you wrote an essay about video games and used these sources. Write the listing for each source. Then, number the entries to show the correct order for a bibliography.

Video Games of Today
By Gloria Carlson

published by
Technology Publishing

_____

_____

_____

Left and Right Brained Games
By Gus Gamer

Game Day Magazine

_____

_____

_____

www.gamersforeverandever.com

Gamers Forever and Ever

Games for the Old and Young
By Carl Player

_____

_____

Tip: Remember that a bibliography should go in alphabetical order by the authors' last names.

WRITING APPLICATION

Description Text Structure

Materials

- copies of *"This Might Make Your Skin Crawl"* (pages 91–92; page91.pdf)
- colored pencils

Procedure

1. Distribute *"This Might Make Your Skin Crawl"* (pages 91–92). Have students read the prompt related to the passage. The prompt is: *Use textual evidence to explain the pros and cons of eyelash mites.*

2. Have students read the text independently and think about how they will answer the prompt.

Student Annotation Focus

While students read, have them use one colored pencil to underline the pros of eyelash mites and another color to underline the cons of eyelash mites.

3. Have students reread the text and annotate as directed.

4. Tell students to use the information from the text to respond to the prompt. You may choose to allow each student to use an additional credible source.

5. Remind students to follow the directions and to use textual evidence and citations.

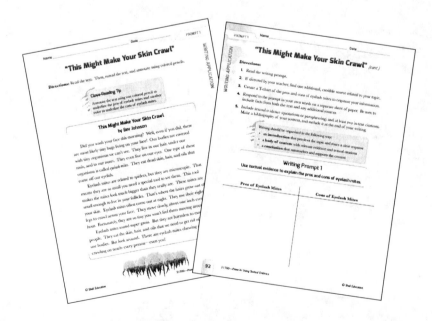

"This Might Make Your Skin Crawl"

Directions: Read the text. Then, reread the text, and annotate using colored pencils.

Close-Reading Tip

Annotate the text using one colored pencil to underline the pros of eyelash mites and another color to underline the cons of eyelash mites.

This Might Make Your Skin Crawl
by Bev Johnson

Did you wash your face this morning? Well, even if you did, there are most likely tiny bugs living on your face! Our bodies are covered with tiny organisms we can't see. They live in our hair, under our nails, and in our noses. They even live on our eyes. One type of these organisms is called *eyelash mites*. They eat dead skin, hair, and oils that come off our eyelids.

Eyelash mites are related to spiders, but they are microscopic. That means they are so small you need a special tool to see them. This tool makes the mites look much bigger than they really are. These mites are small enough to live in your follicles. That's where the hairs grow out of your skin. Eyelash mites often come out at night. They use their eight legs to crawl across your face. They move slowly, about one inch every hour. Fortunately, they are so tiny you won't feel them moving around.

Eyelash mites sound super gross. But they are harmless to most people. They eat the skin, hair, and oils that we need to get rid of from our bodies. But look around. There are eyelash mites chewing and crawling on nearly every person—even you!

page 1

WRITING APPLICATION

"This Might Make Your Skin Crawl" *(cont.)*

Directions

1. Read the writing prompt.

2. If directed by your teacher, find one additional, credible source related to your topic.

3. Create a T-chart of the pros and cons of eyelash mites to organize your information.

4. Respond to the prompt in your own words on a separate sheet of paper. Be sure to include facts from both the text and any additional sources.

5. Include textual evidence (quotations or paraphrasing) and at least two in-text citations. Make a bibliography of your sources, and include it at the end of your writing.

> Writing should be organized in the following way:
>
> • an **introduction** that previews the topic and states a clear claim
> • a **body of content** with relevant evidence and textual citations
> • a **conclusion** that summarizes and supports the claim

Writing Prompt 1

Use textual evidence to explain the pros and cons of eyelash mites.

Pros of Eyelash Mites	Cons of Eyelash Mites

Sequence Text Structure

✏ Materials

- copies of *"Digestion in Depth"* (pages 94–95; page94.pdf)
- colored pencils

Procedure

1. Distribute *"Digestion In Depth"* (pages 94–95). Have students read the prompt related to the passage. The prompt is: *Using the text to support your answer, explain how the digestive system works.*

2. Have students read the text independently and think about how they will answer the prompt.

Student Annotation Focus

While students read, have them use colored pencils to number each basic step.

3. Have students reread the text and annotate as directed.

4. Tell students to use the information from the text to respond to the prompt. You may choose to allow each student to use one additional credible source.

5. Remind students to follow the directions and to use textual evidence and citations.

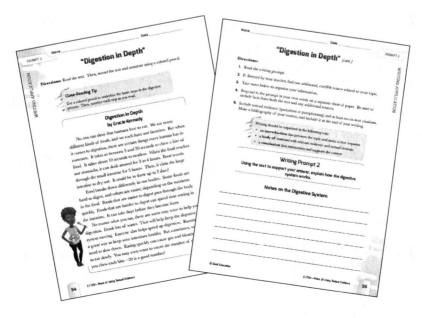

Name _____ Date _____

"Digestion in Depth"

Directions: Read the text. Then, reread the text and annotate using a colored pencil.

Close-Reading Tip

Use a colored pencil to underline the basic steps in the digestive process. Then, number each step as you read.

Digestion in Depth
by Gracie Kennedy

No one can deny that humans love to eat. We eat many different kinds of foods, and we each have our favorites. But when it comes to digestion, there are certain things every human has in common. It takes us between 5 and 30 seconds to chew a bite of food. It takes about 10 seconds to swallow. When the food reaches our stomachs, it can slosh around for 3 to 4 hours. Food travels through the small intestine for 3 hours. Then, it visits the large intestine to dry out. It could be in there up to 2 days!

Food breaks down differently in our bodies. Some foods are hard to digest, and others are easier, depending on the nutrients in the food. Foods that are easier to digest pass through the body quickly. Foods that are harder to digest can spend time rotting in the intestine. It can take days before they become feces.

No matter what you eat, there are some easy ways to help your digestion. Drink lots of water. That will help keep the digestive system moving. Exercise also helps speed up digestion. Running is a great way to keep your intestines healthy. But sometimes, we also need to slow down. Eating quickly can cause gas and bloating. Try to eat slowly. You may even want to count the number of times you chew each bite—20 is a good number!

page 1

"Digestion in Depth" *(cont.)*

Directions

1. Read the writing prompt.

2. If directed by your teacher, find one additional, credible source related to your topic.

3. Take notes below to organize your information.

4. Respond to the prompt in your own words on a separate sheet of paper. Be sure to include facts from both the text and any additional sources.

5. Include textual evidence (quotations or paraphrasing) and at least two in-text citations. Make a bibliography of your sources, and include it at the end of your writing.

Writing should be organized in the following way:

- an **introduction** that previews the topic and states a clear claim
- a **body of content** with relevant evidence and textual citations
- a **conclusion** that summarizes and supports the claim

Writing Prompt 2

Using the text to support your answer, explain how the digestive system works.

Notes on the Digestive System

_____

_____

_____

_____

_____

_____

Compare-and-Contrast Text Structure

🖉 Materials

- copies of *"A Plate for Everyone"* (pages 97–98; page97.pdf)
- colored pencils

Procedure

1. Distribute *"A Plate for Everyone"* (pages 97–98). Have students read the prompt related to the passage. The prompt is: *Use details from the text to compare and contrast vegetarians and vegans.*

2. Have students read the text independently and think about how they will answer the prompt.

Student Annotation Focus

While students read, have them use a colored pencil to underline facts about vegetarians. Have them use a different colored pencil to underline facts about vegans.

3. Have students reread the text and annotate as directed.

4. Tell students to use the information from the text to respond to the prompt. You may choose to allow each student to use one additional credible source.

5. Remind students to follow the directions and to use textual evidence and citations.

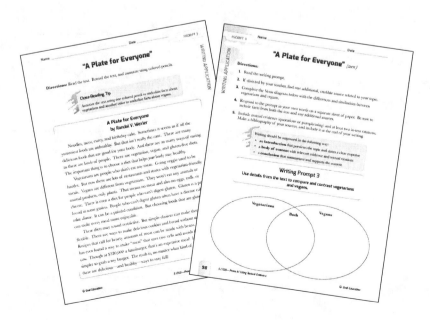

"A Plate for Everyone"

Directions: Read the text. Reread the text, and annotate using colored pencils.

Close-Reading Tip

Annotate the text using one colored pencil to underline facts about vegetarians and another color to underline facts about vegans.

A Plate for Everyone
by Randal V. Wexler

Noodles, tacos, curry, and birthday cake. Sometimes it seems as if all the yummiest foods are unhealthy. But that isn't really the case. There are many delicious foods that are good for your body. And there are as many ways of eating as there are kinds of people. There are vegetarian, vegan, and gluten-free diets. The important thing is to choose a diet that helps *your* body stay healthy.

Vegetarians are people who don't eat any meat. Going veggie used to be harder. But now there are lots of restaurants and stores with vegetarian-friendly meals. Vegans are different from vegetarians. They won't eat any animals or animal products, only plants. That means no meat and also no eggs, milk, or cheese. There is even a diet for people who can't digest gluten. Gluten is a protein found in some grains. People who can't digest gluten often have a disease called *celiac disease*. It can be a painful condition. But choosing foods that are gluten free can make every meal more enjoyable.

These diets may sound restrictive. But simple choices can make them more flexible. There are ways to make delicious cookies and bread without using gluten. Recipes that call for hearty amounts of meat can be made with beans. And science has even found a way to make "meat" that uses cow cells and avoids harming the cow. Though at $330,000 a hamburger, that's an expensive meal! It might be simpler to grab a soy burger. The truth is, no matter what kind of diet you choose, there are delicious—and healthy—ways to stay full!

page 1

WRITING APPLICATION

"A Plate for Everyone" *(cont.)*

Directions

1. Read the writing prompt.

2. If directed by your teacher, find one additional, credible source related to your topic.

3. Complete the Venn diagram below with the differences and similarities between vegetarians and vegans.

4. Respond to the prompt in your own words on a separate sheet of paper. Be sure to include facts from both the text and any additional sources.

5. Include textual evidence (quotations or paraphrasing) and at least two in-text citations. Make a bibliography of your sources, and include it at the end of your writing.

> Writing should be organized in the following way:
>
> • an **introduction** that previews the topic and states a clear claim
> • a **body of content** with relevant evidence and textual citations
> • a **conclusion** that summarizes and supports the claim

Writing Prompt 3

Use details from the text to compare and contrast vegetarians and vegans.

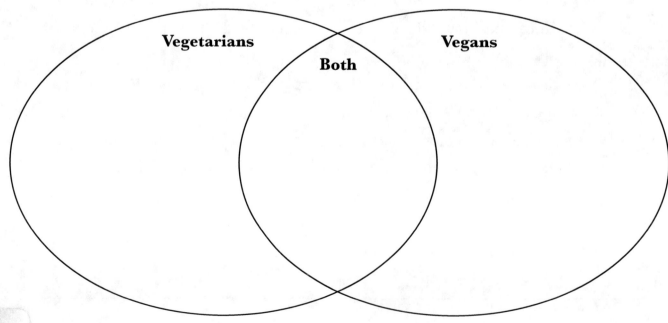

Compare-and-Contrast Text Structure

 Materials

- copies of *"Earthquake Strikes as Locals Sleep"* and *"Earthquake!"* (pages 100–101; page100.pdf)
- colored pencils

Procedure

1. Distribute *"Earthquake Strikes as Locals Sleep"* and *"Earthquake!"* (pages 100–101). Have students read the prompt related to the passage. The prompt is: *Use evidence from the text to define the similarities and differences between the two passages.*

2. Have students read the text independently and think about how they will answer the prompt.

Student Annotation Focus

While students read the two passages, have them circle the similarities and underline the differences with colored pencils.

3. Assign the writing prompt on page 101.

4. Have students use the information from the text to respond to the prompt. You may choose to allow each student to use one additional credible source.

5. Remind students to follow the directions and to use textual evidence and citations.

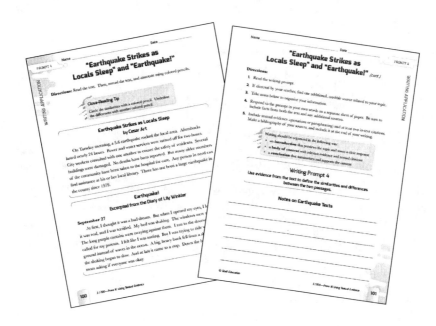

Name _____ Date _____

"Earthquake Strikes as Locals Sleep" and "Earthquake!"

Directions: Read the text. Then, reread the text, and annotate using colored pencils.

Close-Reading Tip

Circle the similarities with a colored pencil. Underline the differences with another colored pencil.

Earthquake Strikes as Locals Sleep
by Cesar Art

On Tuesday morning, a 5.6 earthquake rocked the local area. Aftershocks lasted nearly 24 hours. Power and water services were turned off for two hours. City workers consulted with one another to ensure the safety of residents. Several buildings were damaged. No deaths have been reported. But many older members of the community have been taken to the hospital for care. Any person in need can find assistance at his or her local library. There has not been a large earthquake in the county since 1979.

page 1

Earthquake!
Excerpted from the Diary of Lily Winkler

September 27

At first, I thought it was a bad dream. But when I opened my eyes, I knew it was real, and I was terrified. My bed was shaking. The windows were rattling. The long purple curtains were swaying against them. I ran to the doorway and called for my parents. I felt like I was surfing. But I was trying to ride waves on the ground instead of waves in the ocean. A big, heavy book fell from a shelf. Finally, the shaking began to slow. And at last it came to a stop. Down the hall, I heard my mom asking if everyone was okay.

page 1

"Earthquake Strikes as Locals Sleep" and "Earthquake!" *(cont.)*

Directions

1. Read the writing prompt.

2. If directed by your teacher, find one additional, credible source related to your topic.

3. Take notes below to organize your information.

4. Respond to the prompt in your own words on a separate sheet of paper. Be sure to include facts from both the text and any additional sources.

5. Include textual evidence (quotations or paraphrasing) and at least two in-text citations. Make a bibliography of your sources, and include it at the end of your writing.

Writing should be organized in the following way:

- an **introduction** that previews the topic and states a clear claim
- a **body of content** with relevant evidence and textual citations
- a **conclusion** that summarizes and supports the claim

Writing Prompt 4

Use evidence from the text to define the similarities and differences between the two passages.

Notes on Earthquake Texts

_____

_____

_____

_____

_____

Cause-and-Effect Text Structure

 Materials

- copies of *Excerpt from "History's Mysteries, Vanishing Act"* (pages 103–104; page103.pdf)
- colored pencils

Procedure

1. Distribute *Excerpt from "History's Mysteries, Vanishing Act"* (pages 103–104). Have students read the prompt related to the passage. The prompt is: *Using support from the text, explain the causes of several disappearances of people in the Bermuda Triangle over the years.*

2. Have students read the text independently and think about how they will answer the prompt.

Student Annotation Focus

While students read, have them use colored pencils to underline information that could be related to the causes of the disappearances. Have students write thoughts they may have about the vanishing people, boats, or planes in the margins of the text.

3. Assign the writing prompt on page 104.

4. Have students use the information from the text to respond to the prompt. You may choose to allow each student to use one additional credible source.

5. Remind students to follow the directions and to use textual evidence and citations.

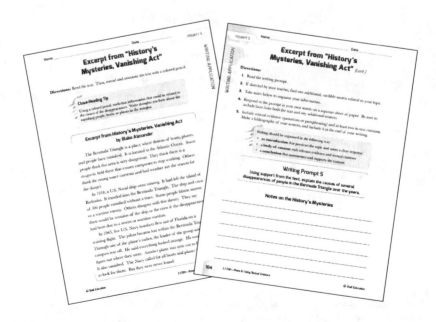

Excerpt from "History's Mysteries, Vanishing Act"

Directions: Read the text. Then, reread and annotate the text with a colored pencil.

Close-Reading Tip

Using a colored pencil, underline information that could be related to the causes of the disappearances. Write thoughts you have about the vanishing people, boats, or planes in the margins.

Excerpt from "History's Mysteries, Vanishing Act"
by Blake Alexander

The Bermuda Triangle is a place where dozens of boats, planes, and people have vanished. It is located in the Atlantic Ocean. Some people think this area is very dangerous. They think there is a magnetic field there that causes compasses to stop working. Others think the strong water currents and bad weather are the reason for the danger.

In 1918, a U.S. Naval ship went missing. It had left the island of Barbados. It traveled into the Bermuda Triangle. The ship and crew of 306 people vanished without a trace. Some people blame storms or a wartime enemy. Others disagree with this theory. They say there would be remains of the ship or the crew if the disappearance had been due to a storm or wartime combat.

In 1945, five U.S. Navy bombers flew out of Florida on a training flight. The pilots became lost within the Bermuda Triangle. Through one of the plane's radios, the leader of the group said his compass was off. He said everything looked strange. He couldn't figure out where they were. Another plane was sent out to find them. It also vanished. The Navy called for all boats and planes in the area to look for them. But they were never found.

page 1

WRITING APPLICATION

Excerpt from "History's Mysteries, Vanishing Act" *(cont.)*

Directions

1. Read the writing prompt.

2. If directed by your teacher, find one additional, credible source related to your topic.

3. Take notes below to organize your information.

4. Respond to the prompt in your own words on a separate sheet of paper. Be sure to include facts from both the text and any additional sources.

5. Include textual evidence (quotations or paraphrasing) and at least two in-text citations. Make a bibliography of your sources, and include it at the end of your writing.

> Writing should be organized in the following way:
> - an **introduction** that previews the topic and states a clear claim
> - a **body of content** with relevant evidence and textual citations
> - a **conclusion** that summarizes and supports the claim

Writing Prompt 5

Using support from the text, explain the causes of several disappearances of people in the Bermuda Triangle over the years.

Notes on the History's Mysteries

_____

_____

_____

_____

_____

Description Text Structure

✏ Materials

- copies of *Excerpt from "All About Sharks"* (pages 106–107; page106.pdf)
- colored pencils

Procedure

1. Distribute *Excerpt from "All About Sharks"* (pages 106–107). Have students read the prompt related to the passage. The prompt is: *Use examples from the text to describe various shark characteristics.*

2. Have students read the text independently and think about how they will answer the prompt.

Student Annotation Focus

While students read, have them identify features that sharks have and underline the details with colored pencils. Additionally, have students circle the adjectives that help identify shark parts.

3. Assign the writing prompt on page 107.

4. Have students use the information from the text to respond to the prompt. You may choose to allow each student to use one additional credible source.

5. Remind students to follow the directions and to use textual evidence and citations.

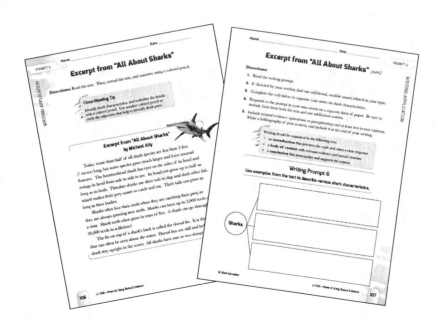

WRITING APPLICATION

Excerpt from "All About Sharks"

Directions: Read the text. Then, reread the text, and annotate using a colored pencil.

Close-Reading Tip

Identify shark characteristics, and underline the details with a colored pencil. Use another colored pencil to circle the adjectives that help to identify shark parts.

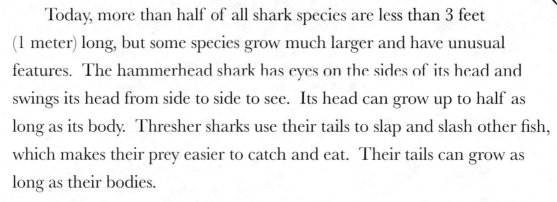

Excerpt from "All About Sharks"
by Michael Ally

Today, more than half of all shark species are less than 3 feet (1 meter) long, but some species grow much larger and have unusual features. The hammerhead shark has eyes on the sides of its head and swings its head from side to side to see. Its head can grow up to half as long as its body. Thresher sharks use their tails to slap and slash other fish, which makes their prey easier to catch and eat. Their tails can grow as long as their bodies.

Sharks often lose their teeth when they are catching their prey, so they are always growing new teeth. Sharks can have up to 3,000 teeth at a time. Shark teeth often grow in rows of five. A shark can go through 30,000 teeth in a lifetime!

The fin on top of a shark's back is called the dorsal fin. It is this fin that can often be seen above the water. Dorsal fins are stiff and help the shark stay upright in the water. All sharks have one or two dorsal fins.

page 1

Excerpt from "All About Sharks" *(cont.)*

Directions

1. Read the writing prompt.

2. If directed by your teacher, find one additional, credible source related to your topic.

3. Complete the web below to organize your notes on shark characteristics.

4. Respond to the prompt in your own words on a separate sheet of paper. Be sure to include facts from both the text and any additional sources.

5. Include textual evidence (quotations or paraphrasing) and at least two in-text citations. Make a bibliography of your sources, and include it at the end of your writing.

> Writing should be organized in the following way:
> - an **introduction** that previews the topic and states a clear claim
> - a **body of content** with relevant evidence and textual citations
> - a **conclusion** that summarizes and supports the claim

Writing Prompt 6

Use examples from the text to describe various shark characteristics.

Sharks

Problem-and-Solution Text Structure

Materials

- copies of *"Welcome to the Desert"* (pages 109–110; page109.pdf)
- colored pencils

Procedure

1. Distribute *"Welcome to the Desert"* (pages 109–110). Have students read the prompt related to the passage. The prompt is: *Using examples from the text, describe possible solutions to problems that could occur in the desert.*

2. Have students read the text independently and think about how they will answer the prompt.

Student Annotation Focus

While students read, have them identify problems that can occur in the desert and underline them with a colored pencil. Have them use a different colored pencil to underline possible solutions.

3. Assign the writing prompt on page 110.

4. Have students use the information from the text to respond to the prompt. You may choose to allow each student to use one additional credible source.

5. Remind students to follow the directions and to use textual evidence and citations.

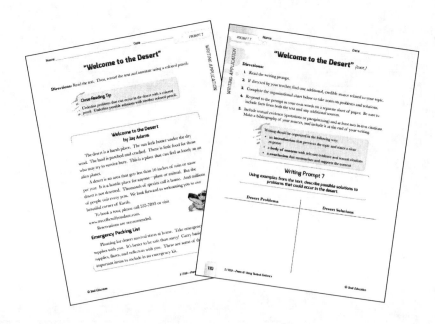

"Welcome to the Desert"

Directions: Read the text. Then, reread the text and annotate using a colored pencil.

Close-Reading Tip

Underline problems that can occur in the desert with a colored pencil. Underline possible solutions with another colored pencil.

Welcome to the Desert
by Jay Adams

The desert is a harsh place. The sun feels hotter under the dry wind. The land is parched and cracked. There is little food for those who may try to survive here. This is a place that can feel as lonely as an alien planet.

A desert is an area that gets less than 10 inches of rain or snow per year. It is a hostile place for anyone—plant or animal. But the desert is not deserted. Thousands of species call it home. And millions of people visit every year. We look forward to welcoming you to our beautiful corner of Earth.

To book a tour, please call 555-7893 or visit www.travelhereifyoudare.com.

Reservations are recommended.

Emergency Packing List

Planning for desert survival starts at home. Take emergency supplies with you. It's better to be safe than sorry! Carry basic medical supplies, flares, and reflectors with you. These are some of the most important items to include in an emergency kit.

page 1

Name _____ Date _____

WRITING APPLICATION

"Welcome to the Desert" *(cont.)*

Directions

1. Read the writing prompt.

2. If directed by your teacher, find one additional, credible source related to your topic.

3. Complete the organizational chart below to take notes on problems and solutions.

4. Respond to the prompt in your own words on a separate sheet of paper. Be sure to include facts from both the text and any additional sources.

5. Include textual evidence (quotations or paraphrasing) and at least two in-text citations. Make a bibliography of your sources, and include it at the end of your writing.

Writing should be organized in the following way:

- an **introduction** that previews the topic and states a clear claim
- a **body of content** with relevant evidence and textual citations
- a **conclusion** that summarizes and supports the claim

Writing Prompt 7

Using examples from the text, describe possible solutions to problems that could occur in the desert.

Desert Problems	Desert Solutions

Chronological Text Structure

✏️ Materials

- copies of *"Skating through History"* (pages 112–113; page112.pdf)
- colored pencils

Procedure

1. Distribute *"Skating through History"* (pages 112–113). Have students read the prompt related to the passage. The prompt is: *Use the text to explain how skateboarding has changed over time.*

2. Have students read the text independently and think about how they will answer the prompt.

Student Annotation Focus

While students read, have them use colored pencils to circle dates. Have students underline information that corresponds with the dates in the same color. Then, have them circle transition words in another color.

3. Assign the writing prompt on page 113.

4. Have students use the information from the text to respond to the prompt. You may choose to allow each student to use one additional credible source.

5. Remind students to follow the directions and to use textual evidence and citations.

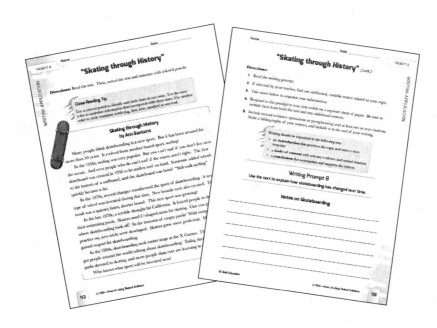

WRITING APPLICATION

Name _____ **Date** _____

"Skating through History"

Directions: Read the text. Then, reread the text and annotate with colored pencils.

Close-Reading Tip

Use a colored pencil to identify and circle dates in one color. Use the same color to underline information that corresponds with those dates. Use another color to circle transition words (e.g., first, next, another) as you read.

Skating through History
by Ann Bantams

Many people think skateboarding is a new sport. But it has been around for more than 50 years. It evolved from another board sport: surfing!

In the 1950s, surfing was very popular. But you can't surf if you don't live near the ocean. And even people who do can't surf if the waves aren't right. The first skateboard was created in 1958 to let surfers surf on land. Someone added wheels to the bottom of a surfboard, and the skateboard was born! "Sidewalk surfing" quickly became a hit.

In the 1970s, several changes transformed the sport of skateboarding. A new type of wheel was invented during this time. New boards were also created. The result was a quieter, faster, shorter board. This new sport was growing!

In the late 1970s, a terrible drought hit California. It forced people to drain their swimming pools. Skaters need U-shaped areas for skating. Can you guess where skateboarding took off? In the bottoms of empty pools! With ramps to practice on, new tricks were developed. Skaters grew more proficient. More people gained respect for skateboarding.

In the 1990s, skateboarding took center stage at the X Games. These games got people around the world talking about skateboarding. Today, there are whole parks devoted to skating, and more people than ever are learning to sidewalk surf.

Who knows what sport will be invented next!

page 1

"Skating through History" *(cont.)*

Directions

1. Read the writing prompt.

2. If directed by your teacher, find one additional, credible source related to your topic.

3. Take notes below to organize your information.

4. Respond to the prompt in your own words on a separate sheet of paper. Be sure to include facts from both the text and any additional sources.

5. Include textual evidence (quotations or paraphrasing) and at least two in-text citations. Make a bibliography of your sources, and include it at the end of your writing.

Writing should be organized in the following way:

- an **introduction** that previews the topic and states a clear claim
- a **body of content** with relevant evidence and textual citations
- a **conclusion** that summarizes and supports the claim

Writing Prompt 8

Use the text to explain how skateboarding has changed over time.

Notes on Skateboarding

_____

_____

_____

_____

_____

_____

Classification Text Structure

✎ Materials

- copies of *Excerpt from "Food Groups"* (pages 115–116; page115.pdf)
- colored pencils

Procedure

1. Distribute *Excerpt from "Food Groups"* (pages 115–116). Have students read the prompt related to the passage. The prompt is: *Using details from the text, identify the four food groups mentioned, and explain why they are important to a person's health.*

2. Have students read the text independently and think about how they will answer the prompt.

Student Annotation Focus

While students read, have them use different colored pencils to underline the important information for each category.

3. Assign the writing prompt on page 116.

4. Have students use the information from the text to respond to the prompt. You may choose to allow each student to use one additional credible source.

5. Remind students to follow the directions and to use textual evidence and citations.

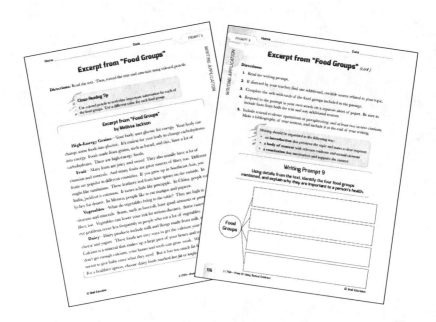

Excerpt from "Food Groups"

Directions: Read the text. Then, reread the text and annotate using colored pencils.

Close-Reading Tip

Use colored pencils to underline important information for each of the food groups. Use a different color for each food group.

Excerpt from "Food Groups"
by Melissa Jackson

High-Energy Grains—Your body uses glucose for energy. Your body can change some foods into glucose. It's easiest for your body to change carbohydrates into energy. Foods made from grains, such as bread and rice, have a lot of carbohydrates. These are high-energy foods.

Fruit—Many fruits are juicy and sweet! They also usually have a lot of vitamins and minerals. And many fruits are great sources of fiber, too. Different fruits are popular in different countries. If you grew up in Southeast Asia, you might like rambutans. These leathery red fruits have spines on the outside. In India, jackfruit is common. It tastes a little like pineapple. In China, people eat lychee for dessert. In Mexico, people like to eat mangos and papaya.

Vegetables—What do vegetables bring to the table? They are high in vitamins and minerals. Some, such as broccoli, have good amounts of protein and fiber, too. Vegetables can lower your risk for serious diseases. Some cancers and eye problems occur less frequently in people who eat a lot of vegetables.

Dairy—Dairy products include milk and things made from milk, such as cheese and yogurt. These foods are easy ways to get the calcium your body needs. Calcium is a mineral that makes up a large part of your bones and teeth. If you don't get enough calcium, your bones and teeth can grow weak. Whole milk is meant to give baby cows what they need. But it has too much fat for many people. For a healthier option, choose dairy foods marked *low fat* or *nonfat*.

page 1

Excerpt from "Food Groups" *(cont.)*

Directions

1. Read the writing prompt.

2. If directed by your teacher, find one additional, credible source related to your topic.

3. Complete the web with each of the food groups included in the passage.

4. Respond to the prompt in your own words on a separate sheet of paper. Be sure to include facts from both the text and any additional sources.

5. Include textual evidence (quotations or paraphrasing) and at least two in-text citations. Make a bibliography of your sources, and include it at the end of your writing.

Writing should be organized in the following way:

- an **introduction** that previews the topic and states a clear response
- a **body of content** with relevant evidence and textual citations
- a **conclusion** that summarizes and supports the content

Writing Prompt 9

Using details from the text, identify the four food groups mentioned, and explain why they are important to a person's health.

Food Groups

Sequence Text Structure

✎ Materials

- copies of *Excerpt from "Pocahontas"* (pages 118–119; page118.pdf)
- colored pencils

Procedure

1. Distribute *Excerpt from "Pocahontas"* (pages 118–119). Have students read the prompt related to the passage. The prompt is: *Use details from the text to tell the sequence of events that led up to Pocahontas's marriage.*

2. Have students read the text independently and think about how they will answer the prompt.

Student Annotation Focus

While students read, have them use different colored pencils for each paragraph as they circle important dates and underline important events.

3. Assign the writing prompt on page 119.

4. Have students use the information from the text to respond to the prompt. You may choose to allow each student to use one additional credible source.

5. Remind students to follow the directions and to use textual evidence and citations.

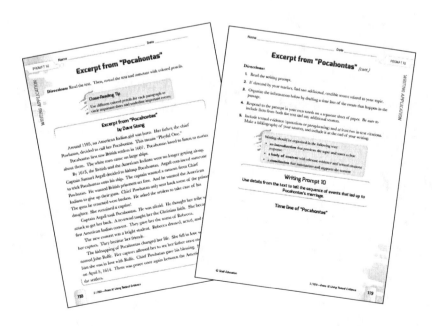

Name _____ Date _____

Excerpt from "Pocahontas"

Directions: Read the text. Then, reread the text and annotate with colored pencils.

Close-Reading Tip

Use different colored pencils for each paragraph to circle important dates and underline important events.

Excerpt from "Pocahontas"
by Dave Stang

Around 1595, an American Indian girl was born. Her father, the chief Powhatan, decided to call her Pocahontas. This means "Playful One."

Pocahontas first saw British settlers in 1607. Pocahontas loved to listen to stories about them. The white men came on large ships.

By 1613, the British and the American Indians were no longer getting along. Captain Samuel Argall decided to kidnap Pocahontas. Argall convinced someone to trick Pocahontas onto his ship. The captain wanted a ransom from Chief Powhatan. He wanted British prisoners set free. And he wanted the American Indians to give up their guns. Chief Powhatan only sent back some of the prisoners. The guns he returned were broken. He asked the settlers to take care of his daughter. She remained a captive!

Captain Argall took Pocahontas. He was afraid. He thought her tribe would attack to get her back. A reverend taught her the Christian faith. She became the first American Indian convert. They gave her the name of Rebecca.

The new convert was a bright student. Rebecca dressed, acted, and prayed like her captors. They became her friends.

The kidnapping of Pocahontas changed her life. She fell in love with a man named John Rolfe. Her captors allowed her to see her father once more. She told him she was in love with Rolfe. Chief Powhatan gave his blessing. She got married on April 5, 1614. There was peace once again between the American Indians and the settlers.

Excerpt from "Pocahontas" *(cont.)*

Directions

1. Read the writing prompt.

2. If directed by your teacher, find one additional, credible source related to your topic.

3. Organize the information below by drafting a time line of the events that happen in the passage.

4. Respond to the prompt in your own words on a separate sheet of paper. Be sure to include facts from both the text and any additional sources.

5. Include textual evidence (quotations or paraphrasing) and at least two in-text citations. Make a bibliography of your sources, and include it at the end of your writing.

> Writing should be organized in the following way:
> - an **introduction** that previews the topic and states a clear claim
> - a **body of content** with relevant evidence and textual citations
> - a **conclusion** that summarizes and supports the claim

Writing Prompt 10

Use details from the text to tell the sequence of events that led up to Pocahontas's marriage.

Time line of "Pocahontas"

_____

Appendices

Appendix A: Answer Key...122
Appendix B: Additional Resources..126
    Text Evidence Vocabulary 126
    Direct Quotations Text Evidence Starters 127
    Paraphrasing Text Evidence Starters 128
    Rubrics 129
    MLA Citing Source Reference 131
    Citing Textual Evidence Posters 132
    Quotation Mark Rules 134
    Reading Levels for Texts 135
Appendix C: Contents of the Digital Resources.......................136
Appendix D: References Cited..136

Answer Key

There are many open-ended questions and writing prompts in this book. For those activities, the answers provided here are examples.

Textual Evidence in Reading

Lesson 1

Matching (page 17)

1. D; 2. A; 3. E; 4. C; 5. B

True/False (page 19)

1. True; 2. False; 3. False; 4. True; 5. True.

Lesson 2

"Take to the Sky" (page 22)

1. In parasailing, a person "wears a parachute and sits on a boat" (Shale 1). Hang gliding is where people "jumps off cliffs to achieve liftoff" (Shale 1).

2. Zip-lining was first created because "people needed a way to quickly get from one place to another" (Shale 1).

"Underwater Architect" (page 23)

1. The bottom of the nautilus shell is lightly colored so that it "blends in with the light coming from above the water" (Shell 1).

2. Beatrice Shell says that "snails and hermit crabs" (1) also have shells to protect them.

Lesson 3

Excerpt from "The Story of Dr. Dolittle" (page 25)

1. This story could not be a true story because the author has animals as main characters who know how to talk, have conversations with humans, and who do human things like sitting around the fire and opening doors (Lofting 1).

2. You can tell the Doctor likes animals because he is spending time with them around a fire and has even written books "in animal language" (Lofting 1).

Excerpt from "Playing for Keeps" (page 26)

1. He is jealous because hi friend geets to play video games at night (Board1).

2. They decide not to play video games because they surprise themselves and want to play board games (Board 1).

Lesson 4

Excerpt from "The Time Machine" (page 28)

1. The author tells us that "it was the Psychologist himself who sent forth the model Time Machine" (Wells par. 3).

"The Key" (page 29)

1. Mary cannot use the key to garden because she isn't sure where the entrance to the garden is. The author explains that she has to "find out where the door [is]" (Burnett par. 1) before she can open it.

Reading Application Practice

Asking Questions—"Man's Best Friend" (page 36)

1. The story, "Man's Best Friend," is written to inform the reader. The first line of the story states, "Dogs have lived closely with humans for thousands of years" (Bernard. 1). The author is not creating a made-up story.

2. According to Bernard, the stories of dogs of the past are based on myths. "In a Norse myth, two dogs chased the sun and moon across the sky" (Bernard 1). This is unrealistic and unlike any dog in today's world.

3. Dogs are referred to as "creatures…connected with another powerful force: death" (Bernard 1). It goes on to state that a three-headed dog guards the dead. Dogs are known for playing, not sitting around watching dead people, which makes this story completely unrealistic.

Answer Key *(cont.)*

Identifying Key Details—"A Cry for Help" (page 40)

1. Pena has been to the cove many times before. The story states, "But this time was different. The air was still, and when she ducked her head under water, she saw a strange light she had never seen before" (Cantell 1). A person can sense when there is something different about a place they have visited time and time again.

2. Pena seems to be a very curious girl. When she notices things are different in the cove, she stays and even ventures out into the water when she sees "a strange light she had never seen before" and "heard someone singing" (Cantell 1). Most people would leave, especially if they heard singing under the water.

3. Pena comes across mermaids in a cove who ask for help and look at her with desperation. According to the author, "Pena didn't know it yet, but she was their only chance for survival" (Cantell 1). The author is foreshadowing adventure.

Making Inferences—"From 613 King Street to Room 4F" (page 44)

1. Taylor must be going through some hard times because the narrator states, "Maybe it will help you," I whisper. "Because I get it—this is hard." (Cobb 1). As the narrator continues, he or she is explaining how his/her life changed from having everything to living in a motel. This must be a connection to Taylor's situation.

2. The narrator is not happy about going from living in a nice house with lots of comforts to a "dirty motel." He or she mentions, "It's hard not having stuff other kids do…" (Cobb 1), but goes on to say loving his or her parents is what matters most. The narrator shows that he or she is a caring person by trying to lift Taylor's spirits.

3. The narrator is not happy about his/her current situation. The narrator states, "My family used to be wealthy, but not anymore, and I can't stand it." (Cobb 1). He/she goes on to tell Taylor about the changes that have occurred. Then, he/she offers hope that things will get better, but you can tell that the narrator is not happy either.

Finding the Moral of the Story—"The Ant and the Chrysalis" (page 48)

1. The moral of this story is that appearances are deceptive. The ant walks around the cocoon and brags, "I can run hither and yonder, here and there. You can go nowhere at all" (Autry 1). When the ant sees what becomes of the creature once it leaves its cocoon, the ant realizes that he should not have said mean things.

2. At first, the chrysalis is unable to talk, so he must listen to the ant's mean words without sticking up for himself. Once the butterfly is out of the cocoon, he tells the ant, "You can crawl on the ground or even up a tree, but without wings, you cannot fly from place to place" (Autry 1). The ant may have done a lot of talking in the beginning, but the butterfly gets the last word.

3. The author writes about how the butterfly "had more freedom than the ant ever would" (Autry 1) because the butterfly is now able to fly and go wherever he wants. The ant, who was mean-spirited, sensed something was up when he "felt a shadow pass over him" (Autry 1) and then realized he was the one with limited abilities.

Determining Figurative Language—"My Shadow" (page 52)

1. Robert Louis Stevenson uses a simile in the stanza, "For he sometimes shoots up taller like an India-rubber ball" (7). The shadow's height is being compared to how high an India-rubber ball can bounce.

2. Stevenson is comparing his shadow to someone that is sleeping in. Because of the time of day, there is no shadow, "One morning, very early, before the sun was up" (13). If it is still dark outside, the shadow is still sleeping.

3. The child seems to be agitated and annoyed with his shadow. "And can only make a fool of me in every sort of way" (Stevenson 10) suggests that the shadow humiliates him. Later, he calls the shadow a "coward" because he never leaves his side. In the end, he seems happy to leave him home on a dark morning.

Answer Key (cont.)

Analyzing Character—"Checkmate"
(page 56)

1. At the beginning of the story, Ayeesha has no knowledge of the game of chess, and over time, she becomes an avid player. Eventually, she even beats her friend and teacher, Ventu. From there, "She works her way through Uganda, beating all the best players" (Greene par. 3). Ayeesha also goes to other countries around the world to play.

2. Ventu's remark comparing winning chess to winning at life means that if Ayeesha can dedicate herself to becoming a champion chess player, she can put the same effort into having a successful life. Her dedication is evident when she "is rushing to finish her chores and walking to the church every day" (Greene par. 2). With that kind of devotion, anything is possible.

3. In the story, "Checkmate," the author uses a metaphor to compare physical hunger to Ayeesha's hunger to improve her personal situation. Her life must not be an easy one, because her friend, Ventu, says, "'In chess, it doesn't matter where you come from. Only where you put the pieces'" (Greene par. 1). Ayeesha's home country is Uganda, which is a nation where much of the population suffers from poverty.

Main Idea—"Go-Kart Racing" (page 60)

1. The main idea of the first paragraph in the text, "Go-Kart Racing," is the different ways go-carts achieve speed. The first sentence states, "The thrill of a go-kart comes from the speed of the ride" (Scott 1). The author proceeds to discuss go-carts' engines, or lack of them, and the many ways to build up speed.

2. The main idea in the second paragraph of the story is braking the go-karts. According to Greene, "They need to be safe as they drive at top speeds" (1), but they can have levers as well. It is important to have a way to stop the go-kart safely so that there are no accidents.

3. The main idea of the text is how a go-kart operates. Greene gives specific details about go-cart races and how they stop. Interestingly, "not all go-karts have engines" (1) some run downhill

with just a push, but luckily, "most go-karts have brake pedals" (1).

Identifying Author's Purpose—"A Beginner's Guide to Soccer" (page 64)

1. The author's purpose is to inform readers about the game of soccer. Biman explains a little about soccer's history and how it is "the most popular sport in the world" (1). It seems as if the author is passionate about the topic of soccer, because he is so knowledgeable and uses exclamation points to express feelings.

2. The picture the author paints in this passage is one of excitement and passion for the game of soccer. Picturing royalty outlawing soccer because "they thought people were getting too angry when they lost games" (Biman 1) is silly to imagine happening. For centuries, soccer has played a big part the sports world, and it doesn't look like it's going to stop any time soon!

3. When soccer was first invented, it started in Asia and was different than today's version. Then, playing soccer consisted of "moving the ball into a small net" (Biman 1). Today, players move the ball to the other team's net without the use of their hands and arms.

Studying Text Structure—"How to Blow Bigger Bubbles" (page 68)

1. This text is informational because it is telling the reader how to make something. The text has a section that contains materials needed and includes six steps such as, "1. Attach an eye screw to one end of each dowel" (Ubble par. 3). These are specific instructions to follow to make bigger bubbles.

2. The directions say to avoid making the bubbles while mixing the water, soap, and glycerin. This could be because the next step is to "place your wand in the bubble solution" (Ubble par. 7) and if there are bubbles present, it may make it difficult for the soap to spread evenly on the cord.

3. The author wrote this passage to give instructions on how to make bigger bubbles. In the beginning, Ubble begins the text with the question, "What's the biggest bubble you've ever blown?" (par. 1). This is great way to grab

Answer Key (cont.)

a reader's attention and introduce a subject to someone who might not care about blowing bubbles. The structure of this text appears to be well-thought out and planned by Ubble.

Comparing and Contrasting—Excerpt from "Circuits" (page 72)

1. Series circuits and parallel circuits are alike because they conduct electricity and use switches to "open and close circuits" (Noah par. 3). They also use pathways for the electricity to travel.

2. There are several differences between series circuits and parallel circuits. A series circuit has only one pathway, while a parallel circuit has more than one. If anything on the path of a series circuit fails, "if one component fails, they all do" (Noah par. 1). If parallel circuits have a bulb or plug go out, the rest of the pathway will continue to work.

3. The example allows readers to visualize what the author is describing about series circuits. The example describes one path where "all the light bulbs are lined up in a series circuit" (Noah par. 2). It is easy to understand how all the bulbs could fail if one stops working.

Textual Evidence in Writing

Lesson 6

Gathering Sources Practice 1 (page 76)

1. books, magazines; 2. websites, online journals; 3. sources that are backed by experts; 4. trusted sources; 5. best family vacation spots; 6. macaroni and cheese recipe; 7. adopting a puppy. 8. Yes; 9. No; 10. No

Gathering Sources Practice 2 (page 77)

Responses for questions 1–4 will vary but should include key words related to the topics; 5. No; 6. Yes; 7. No

Lesson 7

Supporting a Claim Practice 1 (page 79)

1. N; 2. LR; 3. LR; 4. N; 5. RE; 6. LR; 7. LR; 8. RE; 9. LR; 10. RE; 11. LR

Supporting a Claim Practice 2 (page 80)

1. N; 2. LR; 3. LR; 4. LR; 5. N; 6. RE; 7. N; 8. RE; 9. LR

Lesson 8

Organizing Evidence Practice 1 (page 82)

The following is one way the statements could be organized: Topic A: monkeys have crazy behavior (2, 4, 7); Topic B: monkeys take time to care for (1, 5, 9); Topic C: monkeys can be expensive (3, 6, 8)

Organizing Evidence Practice 2 (page 83)

The following is one way the statements could be organized: Topic A: biography basics; Topic B: life as a traveler; Topic C: lived a simple life

Lesson 9

Writing an Analysis Practice 1 (page 86)

Check that the "Reason" column uses evidence from both the text and the student's own ideas.

Writing and Analysis Practice 2 (page 86)

Student essays will vary but should include information from their charts as well as proper citations.

Lesson 10

Listing Sources Practice 1 (page 88)

2. Creature, Buddy. *Strange Bugs*. Allen Publishing; 3. Flyer, Julie. "Big Bugs of the Northwest." *National Bug Magazine*.; 1. Beetle, George. "Bugs Big and Small." www.weirdbugsandinsects.com.

Listing Sources Practice 2 (page 89)

1. Carlson, Gloria. *Video Games of Today*. Technology Publishing.

2. Gamer, Gus. "Left and Right Brained Games." *Game Day*.

3. Player, Carl. "Games for the Old and Young." Gamers for Ever and Ever. www.gamersforeverandever.com

Text Evidence Vocabulary

Word/Phrase	Definition
cite	to quote or paraphrase from text to help support or prove a claim
credible sources	sources the reader can trust and believe because they are authored or published by a reputable person or organization that uses research as evidence
direct quotation	the exact words of someone else woven into your writing, noted by using quotation marks
in-text citations	stating the author and page or paragraph number from a source when using a direct quotation or paraphrasing
logical reasoning	statements that are written by the author that prove their claim makes sense
paraphrasing	restatement or rewording of an idea from a text
plagiarism	the practice of taking someone else's work and passing it off as your own
preferred style	a specialized way of ordering punctuation, grammar, and in-text citations from a specific set of guidelines
relevant evidence	facts that come from sources
relevant sources	sources that relate to the topic of a piece of writing
source	a place where information on a topic is gathered
text	the original piece of writing being cited
textual evidence	noting evidence from a text to help with proving an argument, or claim

Direct Quotations
Text Evidence Starters

✏️ **The author states...**

✏️ **The author tells us that...**

✏️ **According to the text...**

✏️ **In paragraph _____, it says...**

✏️ **For instance, the text states...**

✏️ **When the author states...**

✏️ **One example from the text is...**

Paraphrasing Text
Evidence Starters

✐ **Based on the text...**

✐ **The author explains that...**

✐ **When the author describes...**

✐ **The author implies that...**

✐ **From the reading, we can tell that...**

✐ **For instance, the text explains that...**

✐ **For example, the text describes...**

Close-Reading Annotations Rubric

	3 points Quality	2 points Developing	1 point Approaching
Quality/Comprehension	Annotations show a thorough analysis of the text. **Indicators** • higher-level questions • key vocabulary questioned or identified • inferential comments • displays depth of thinking • clear attention to close-reading lesson focus	Annotations show some analysis of the text. **Indicators** • basic questions • key vocabulary questioned • some inferential thinking, but most comments are concrete • comments only occasionally show depth • attempts to attend to close-reading lesson focus	Annotations show little or no analysis of the text. **Indicators** • demonstrates little understanding of the text with unrelated comments • comments often restate text • comments are only concrete • little or no attempt at close-reading lesson focus
Quantity	5–8 annotations	3–4 annotations	0–2 annotations

Citing Textual Evidence in Writing Rubric

	3 points Quality	2 points Developing	1 point Approaching
State Claim	The claim is clearly stated and applicable to the topic.	The claim is stated but may be unclear.	The topic is stated, but the claim is unclear or missing.
Evidence	Evidence from sources accurately responds to and supports the claim through direct quotations or paraphrasing.	Evidence from sources stays on topic, but its origin is unclear.	Evidence is not included or is inaccurate or unsupportive of claim.
Explanation of Claim	An analysis and explanation strongly connect to and support the claim.	An explanation of the claim is provided with some analysis or support.	There is little to no attempt at explaining the claim.
In-Text Citation and Document Sources	Citations of evidence are correctly provided; when applicable, sources are accurately documented.	Citations of evidence are sometimes provided; when applicable, sources are listed but may not include information needed.	Citations of evidence are attempted but may be inaccurate; even when applicable, sources are not listed.
Research	Sources are highly relevant to the topic and credible.	Sources are somewhat relevant to the topic and somewhat credible.	Sources are missing or are used but may not be relevant or credible.

MLA Citing Source Reference

Standard Format of Citing within a Sentence	
Direct Quotation	**Paraphrasing**
Example using author with paragraph number: According to Smith, "Automobile accidents are the number one cause of deaths for teenagers ages 15–20" (par. 1). with page number: According to Smith, "Automobile accidents are the number one cause of deaths for teenagers ages 15–20" (1). **Example using name of article** with paragraph number: According to the article, "Teen Accident Statistics," "Automobile accidents are the number one cause of deaths for teenagers ages 15–20" (par. 1). with page number: According to the article, "Teen Accident Statistics," "Automobile accidents are the number one cause of deaths for teenagers ages 15–20" (1).	**Original Passage:** There was a time when most teens were counting down to their 16th birthday. Nothing was more important than getting that key to freedom: the coveted driver's license. Acquiring a driver's license was much more important a generation ago, but no more. Driving a car used to be "cool" and a status symbol, but times have changed, and having a car doesn't have the same appeal as it did then. ("Priorities Are Changing" par. 1) **Acceptable Paraphrase:** When reading the article, "Priorities Are Changing," it is clear to see that being a teen driver and having a car are not as "cool" as they used to be.

Standard Format of Citing at the End of a Sentence	
Direct Quotation	**Paraphrasing**
Example using author with paragraph number: "Automobile accidents are the number one cause of deaths for teenagers ages 15–20" (Smith par.1). with page number: "Automobile accidents are the number one cause of deaths for teenagers ages 15–20" (Smith 1). **Example using name of article** with paragraph number: "Automobile accidents are the number one cause of deaths for teenagers ages 15–20" ("Teen Accident Statistics" par. 1). with page number: "Automobile accidents are the number one cause of deaths for teenagers ages 15–20" ("Teen Accident Statistics" 1).	**Original Passage:** There was a time when most teens were counting down to their 16th birthday. Nothing was more important than getting that key to freedom: the coveted driver's license. Acquiring a driver's license was much more important a generation ago, but no more. Driving a car used to be "cool" and a status symbol, but times have changed, and having a car doesn't have the same appeal as it did then (Smith par. 1). **Acceptable Paraphrase:** Teenagers today are in no hurry to get their driver's licenses. They have different priorities from teens of the past (Smith par.1).

APA is the most commonly used style within social sciences.

MLA is the most commonly used style within humanities.

How to Cite Textual Evidence in Reading

- ✏️ **Accurately ANSWER the question.**

- ✏️ **Provide EVIDENCE from the reading passage to SUPPORT your answer.**

- ✏️ **Correctly CITE the answer with (author and paragraph or page number).**

- ✏️ **Write a final thought to CONNECT or further explain your answer using logical reasoning.**

Steps to Cite Textual Evidence in Writing

1. **State claim.**

   ↓

2. **Explain claim.**

   ↓

3. **Research relevant and credible sources.**

   ↓

4. **Use textual evidence from sources by quoting or paraphrasing.**

   ↓

5. **Use in-text citations and document sources.**

   ↓

6. **Connect or support your claim and evidence with logical reasoning.**

Quotation Mark Rules

Rule	Example
Commas are used to introduce direct quotations.	Carson said, "We need to leave now."
Commas are used to interrupt direct quotations.	"Why," I asked, "what's the hurry?"
If the speech tag (i.e., John said, I asked) is at the end of the sentence, always place a comma before it.	"I can't wait until summer," said Amber.
Capitalize the first word in a direct quotation, unless you are quoting part of the text.	Ava stated in her article, "Solar power is the future." Ava said that our planet, "has a way of taking care of itself."
Use ellipses (…) to represent any missing words.	Ava stated in her article, "…using solar power will benefit mankind."
Ellipses can be place at the beginning or the end of a direct quotation, or both.	Ava stated in her article, "…sun-generated power is a free alternative…."
If a quotation includes a question mark or exclamation mark, place it inside the quotation marks.	Valerian asks in her book, "What has made man want to kill elephant for their tusks?"
If asking a question, place question mark outside the quotation.	Do you believe the saying, "Blood is thicker than water"?
Commas and periods ALWAYS go inside quotation marks.	According to Yahir, "Eating several servings of whole grain a day is healthy for you."

Reading Levels for Texts

Text	Reading Level	Page
"Soccer" by Melinda Ramos	4.5	18
"Giraffes" by Maria Collins	5.9	20
"Take to the Sky" by Jeff Shale	4.2	22
"Underwater Architect" by Beatrice Shell	4.4	23
Excerpt from *The Story of Doctor Dolittle* by Hugh Lofting	5.7	25
Excerpt from "Playing for Keeps" by Carmen Board	2.7	26
Excerpt from *The Time Machine* by H. G. Wells	4.4	28
"The Key"—Adapted from *The Secret Garden* by Frances Hodgson Burnett	4.4	29
"How Are Fossil Fuels Made?" by Andrew Roberts	4.8	31
"It's the Law! But Why?" by Devin Garrison	3.2	32
"Man's Best Friend" by Jason Bernard	4.5	35
"A Cry for Help" by Alice Cantell	4.1	39
"From 613 King Street to Room 4F" by Paul Cobb	3.5	43
"The Ant and the Chrysalis—A Retelling of Aesop's Fable" by Dillon Autry	3.5	47
"My Shadow" by Robert Louis Stevenson	8.4	51
"Checkmate" by Cali Greene	4.1	55
"Go-Kart Racing" by Karl Scott	4.3	59
"A Beginner's Guide to Soccer" by Alex Biman	4.5	63
"How to Blow Bigger Bubbles" by Jacob Ubble	4.6	67
Excerpt from "Circuits" by M. J. Noah	4.9	71
"Should Video Games Be Considered a Sport? "	5.6	79
"Should Graffiti be Considered Art?"	5.2	80
"This Might Make Your Skin Crawl" by Bev Johnson	3.7	91
"Digestion In Depth" by Gracie Kennedy	4.2	94
"A Plate for Everyone" by Randal V. Wexler	5.3	97
"Earthquake Strikes as Locals Sleep" by Cesar Art; "Earthquake!" Excerpted from the Diary of Lily Winkler	4.4	100
Excerpt from "History's Mysteries, Vanishing Act" by Blake Alexander	5.3	103
Excerpt from "All About Sharks" by Michael Ally	4.2	106
"Welcome to the Desert" by Jay Adams	5.5	109
"Skating through History" by Ann Bantams	5.6	112
Excerpt from "Food Groups" by Melissa Jackson	5.3	115
Excerpt from "Pocahontas" by Dave Stang	5.9	118

Contents of the Digital Resources

To access the digital resources, go to this website and enter the following code: **91911001**

www.teachercreatedmaterials.com/administrators/download-files/

The contents of the digital resources is divided into two folders. Below are brief descriptions of each folder's contents.

Student Resources

This folder contains student reproducibles needed for the lessons. The filenames of these pages are included in the materials lists within the lessons. This folder also contains additional student resources, such as the charts and information from the appendices.

Teacher Resources

This folder contains the example student reproducibles. The filenames of these pages are included in the materials lists within the lessons. This folder also contains additional teacher resources, such as the charts and information from the appendices.

References Cited

Atkins, Janet. 2011. "From the Secondary Section: Reading and Writing with Purpose: In and Out of School." *The English Journal* 101(2): 12–13.

Fisher, Douglas B., and Nancy Frey. 2014. *Close Reading and Writing From Sources*. Newark, DE: International Reading Association.

Graham, Steve, and Michael Hebert. 2010. *Writing to Read: Evidence for How Writing Can Improve Reading.* A Carnegie Corporation Time to Act Report. Washington, DC: Alliance for Excellent Education.